Transcending My Brooklyn

4 years in the Middle East

by

Hamza Makonnen

edited by Marlon Rice

Library of Congress Cataloging-in-Publication Data can be obtained from the publisher upon request.

ISBN 978-1-517-78558-1

Manufactured in the United States

About Press & Push Publishing

Press & Push Publishing is a social enterprise geared towards developing and distributing beneficial media for the Hip-Hop generation and greater audience at large. We aim to aid in redefining and legitimatizing Hip-Hop as a culture that will one day will be examined as a vessel which was more than a merely a musical past time and/or a mere subculture for those rebellious few reluctant to conform to mainstream American culture.

TABLE OF CONTENTS

Forward

My Brooklyn is a city within the city of all cities. Despite its official classification as a borough in New York City, native Brooklynites have long inflated the borough's stature locally and across the globe. While most New Yorkers who aren't from Brooklyn merely claim New York when asked about their place of origin, Brooklynites are quite different. We boldly declare, "I'm from Brooklyn" whenever anyone questions us about our hometown. We assume everyone knows where Brooklyn is, which is true because almost everyone does know where Brooklyn is. It was this stout bravado that gave us such a well-known reputation, which many of us have benefited from throughout our lives. Since all good things come to an end, through submersion in a foreign culture deaf to the legend of Brooklyn I found myself anew being forced to transcend all that I have ever known only to awaken with new eyes.

About This Offering

Similar to my first literary endeavor, *"From the Stoop to the Booth"*, the goal of this project was to share my experiences, thoughts, and more importantly my travels with the intent of provoking thought while hopefully motivating change. With this current undertaking, instead of trekking around America as an unsigned rapper as was done in *"From the Stoop to the Booth"*, I relocated to the Middle East with my ex-wife and young daughter for a period of almost four years. Within these pages are epiphanies, observations, and commentary on life in the Middle East and, in general, coming from an urban American perspective.

This book was not written chronologically; rather essays were pieced together from the writings I used as a hobby to keep my mind occupied while enduring some of the trials that come with submersion. Also included are the newer pieces written when I returned. If I were to advise the reader on how to read this book, I would encourage reading the "About Me" piece followed by "4 years an Arab" then go to the table of contents to find a piece that piques your interest.

As a communicator, writer and expressionist, I am not sure if any writer can fully capture the awe-inspiring experience of submersing in a foreign culture. How does one articulate the pungent spices that make the tongue feel as if its been holding back for so many years? Or the astonishment of seeing droves of local men leaving work midday just to watch a soccer match with the approval of their supervisors, as I observed while in Kuwait. Some things do need to be experienced firsthand, however, I dug deep within myself to relay what I could to the best of my ability. My recollections never play back in a time-sequenced manner; rather I remember the events that were the most striking and indelible. Also, while adjusting to being in the Middle East, as well as my reentry and adjustment to being back home, my thoughts were literally scrambled all over the place. Considering these factors, a collection of essays and observations rather an a chronological story of my travels is most fitting.

The goal is to replicate what was felt while relaying the most memorable times and those moments of epic clarity I had while living abroad. In addition, woven into the threads of intent is a notice to Americans, but mostly my Hip-Hop American community, that there are greener pastures outside of America. The earth is quite spacious with various fruits to be reaped, but only those who are courageous enough to take the leap will have the chance to eat. What follows within these pages is Hamza Makonnen transcending all that was known then returning home with new eyes; transcendent.

About Me

My name is Hamza Makonnen. A 2nd generation American of Ethiopian descent, I was born in Brooklyn, New York during the early 80s. At the time my Christian born mother had become a convert to Judaism and involved heavily in the local Pan-African movement. By the time I had reached 3 years old, she converted to Islam then married the man who that would later raise me. Suffice to say, by the age of five my exposure to all things diverse was the norm. While the other young kids from my block were only exposed to the neighborhood and the regular lifestyle found in Brooklyn during the 1980s, my ties with Muslim, Pan-African, Black Jew communities of New York City gave me a broader outlook on life.

In each of my respective communities were individuals, and sometimes, families who migrated abroad due to being displeased with the quality of life in America. The Pan-Africans ventured to West and Central Africa while members from the American Muslim community settled throughout countries with large Islamic populations such as Egypt, Sudan, Malaysia, Morocco, and the Middle East. It was actually a common occurrence for a childhood friend to move to another country. In fact, three of my closest childhood friends left America before I had reached the age of 10; for Sudan, Egypt and Saudi Arabia respectively. From early in life my childhood was very different from most American kids regardless of race and socioeconomic status. The diversity and exposure to paradigms other than the generic "white picket fence" dream would eventually steer me in the direction that landed me in the Arabian Peninsula with my wife, at the time, and our infant daughter.

What led to me to leave? Well, I had visited family that migrated to Saudi Arabia some years prior then instantly fell in love with the option of having other options. Not being bound to a single land was and still is a refreshing alternative, offering a wide new range of possibilities. During my first stay in Saudi Arabia for six weeks in 2008, I experienced a quality of life more

11

conducive to raising a family in safety without being concerned with the violence and normal pitfalls found in the States. In addition, it did not hurt that my mother, a devout Black American Muslim, had immigrated to Saudi Arabia 10 years prior. With an idea of what to expect and a support system already setup, my wife and I made the 15 hour trek across the Atlantic Ocean with baby in tow to start a new life as American expatriates living abroad.

Because I had family there, my transition was almost seamless. I was able to find a nice four bedroom flat close to my mother's home. The flat was palatial with large rooms, marble floors, and intricately designed drop ceilings with tracking lighting. It was a long way away from the railroad apartment in Brooklyn I had rented prior to leaving America. All the doors were sturdy oak wood while the bathroom fixtures were artistic and divinely regal. With a simple plane ride, I upgrade my quality of living tenfold for a fraction of the price. Coming from the hood, that type of opportunity would be called a no-brainer.

Aside from the lavish living accommodations, I had to adjust to the heat which was quite the task. With temperatures averaging 110 degrees Fahrenheit in the summer, water became my closest companion and confidant. Everyday, I drank well over 2 gallons a day with no problem. The heat coupled with the hot, dry breeze of Madinah, one of the two holy cities in Saudi Arabia, made perspiring on uncovered skin virtually impossible. As soon as a bead of sweat would attempt to excrete from the pores on my face it would evaporate. Eventually, I developed acne of sorts that I never had in America. My forehead and cheeks were covered with small blemishes and pimples, which were also probably, caused by the tap water as much as by the severe heat. The city I was residing in at the time did not have underground piping for water in residential areas, so the landlords would fill large tanks on the roofs with water similar to how it was once done long ago in the States. In addition, because there were no underground gas lines, residents had to purchase canisters of gas for the stove in order to cook. This seemed strange, but it soon became clear that most things are strange when submersed in a culture totally different from the culture a person is accustomed to. Considering the wealth of The Kingdom of Saudi I still thought this to be antiquated, however I later learned that only certain cities were without underground piping.

Adjusting to the elements was tough, but not as tough as learning that time travels much slower in Saudi Arabia. Look at it like the difference between a bustling urban metropolis like Manhattan and a suburban cul de sac in Anytown, America. The Saudi pace was a crippled tortoise high on opium: extremely slow. Coming from New York City this initially drove me stir crazy, as I needed everything done immediately while the local attitude was much more relaxed. Eventually, after time had passed I adjusted to the pace as humans often do. The local culture as well as the extreme climate dictated that my New York speed demon attitude would have to be tossed to the side. Again, the weather was a formidable beast that had to be respected lest dehydration and heat exhaustion were welcomed, which they clearly were not.

Due to the extreme heat in Saudi Arabia, many shops closed down for a siesta during the hottest hours of the day. In the beginning, I rejected the idea of a midday nap because New Yorkers do not sleep, but then I constantly found myself utterly drained around 3pm, which in turn forced me to observe the local custom of a siesta. It had seemed the heat had just been too much to bear even for someone who was well hydrated. The midday naps became quite the treat for me. Often I found myself looking forward to my nap time, as if I was suddenly back in nursery as a child.

After the initial hurdles of adjustment had subsided everything else was smooth sailing. In addition to having family there in Saudi, I also had a few childhood friends either attending school or teaching at one of the many local universities. Being able to have dinner with a handful of childhood friends thousands of miles away from home eased things up drastically. However, the fact remained I was still a long away from my Brooklyn in a very unfamiliar place.

There is no easy way to migrate to a foreign country with a culture so different from one's own, but if there ever was an ideal setup, I had it. I understand that that idea of relocating to a different country may be foreign to most Americans, but globally and historically, people have always migrated from their homelands in search of greener pastures. All one has to do is look at the colonist of early America to see this country's founding was in part based on the early settlers trekking across the ocean. Making a home away from home is normal while the current American attitude towards intercontinental relocating is not. Perhaps at the end of this project an interest may be piqued in the reader to step outside of the box and live. I once read somewhere that life begins where one's comfort zone ends. If this holds true my life began when I exited the airplane in Jeddah, Saudi Arabia because I was way out of my comfort zone and I do not regret the experience at all.

Man, Hood, and Beyond

Back when I was a nappy headed, snot-nosed little kid riding my bicycle around Brooklyn an older cousin of mine always encouraged me to travel. This cousin, John-John, was a musician who traveled frequently throughout the world. Africa, Europe, Australia, South America, and every other corner of the Earth, John-John had visited performing as a drummer with his rock band, Living Colour. Whenever he returned home to New York, he would pick me up in his fancy car then drive me around the city to hang out and enjoy the sights. During those weekend excursions to play basketball or go to the shows at the Jacob Javits Center, I distinctly remember him persistently urging me to travel. Though I was only 11 or 12 at the time, he was insistent on drilling the mandate to travel in my head. That advice was rooted in him wanting me to broaden my overall scope of life if only because the the world outlook of a young man coming of age in a drug and violence infested neighborhood is often quite bleak.

One weekend while hanging out with him we went to the now-defunct Tower Records on Broadway in Manhattan. Being that he was a musician, I automatically assumed we were going in the store to purchase new music. My assumption was correct, but what I did not anticipate was that he would be buying foreign music. Astonished and confused, I questioned why and how could he listen to music in languages he could not understand. Though I do not remember his reply verbatim, the answer was to the effect of: not listening for the words, but listening to the rhythm and the feeling of the music.

In retrospect, that was my first lesson in reading between the lines of a foreign culture when the language spoken is not fully understood. That lesson would eventually benefit me greatly when I found myself in an Arab country without command of the local language left to understand the people only by their body language, facial expressions and other visual cues. Though the Arabs were not a Fela Kuti cd, I still had to become adept at "reading in between the lines" in order to understand the locals I came in contact with. In a more general sense, his encouragement to travel had completely pushed me to the other side of the world and his reasoning eventually made even more sense to me the more I experienced the Arab culture.

Long before I had decided to take a job in the Middle East, I was around 16 years old the first time I experienced living in a place far, far away from my Brooklyn comfort zone. It was at that age when I, with my family, moved to the southwest section of London called Brixton. The experience was an adventure that was unforgettable beyond belief. During the time when we had first moved, I was quite reluctant to fully embrace the new experience solely due to the fact the reason for my move was a mother's new husband, who happened to be a British businessman. In my adolescent mind, he moved me away from my friends and stomping grounds, so the only possible reaction was to put up a stubborn protest of sorts. For the first month after the move, I never really left the flat except to go to the corner-store. Eventually, I did leave the flat only to be amazed at what I saw in London.

The neighborhood, Brixton, was supposed to be a rough, tough hood where people were frequently being stabbed and robbed. Coming from a place in New York City where shootings, not stabbings, were the norm, I really did not see too much of a threat, so I ventured and explored Brixton. Seeing the young fashion trendy folks strolling through Brixton Market was very comforting if only due to the fact it reminded me of Brooklyn's Fulton Mall during its heyday. In addition, this was my first time actually living in a real melting pot. During that period in the mid 1990s, despite New York City being called a melting pot the area that I had lived in, Bed-Stuy, was predominantly Black with no real diversity. There were a sprinkles of Latino families and a few white folk peppered throughout, but Bed-Stuy was, in large, a Black neighborhood.

After getting my feet wet in and around Brixton, I was soon window-shopping and exploring to see what the rest of London had to offer in regards to clothing, footwear, sights and pretty girls. Eventually, I was introduced to the British slang, which called sneakers: trainers. Yes, Nike, Reebok, Adidas, etc. were referred to as trainers even though I rarely bought sneakers for the purpose of training. As the sneaker experts would agree: Sneakers are meant for style purposes even before their intended athletic use. During those sneaker-hunting days is when I was first made aware of how currency converts. While searching for a pair sneakers I noticed, what I thought to be, a price similarity between the UK and the US. A pair of nice sneakers cost $120 in the US while in the UK the same pair costs 120 pound. Initially, I had thought the prices were the same until I did a conversion then realized 120 pound was actually around $180. Needless to say, I did not purchase any sneakers while in the UK, but instead I had my family in the States send them to me. The prices were just excessively expensive for my limited funds.

Eventually, I had also befriended a few guys on the local basketball team which was similar to the AAU circuit in America. That also aided in me settling down because it brought even more familiarity to the experience of living in a foreign country. Since I was an avid basketball player during my teens, being able to partake in my favorite past time while being in an unfamiliar place eased my nerves making me forget about being away from home. After a while Brixton had become a home to me and despite missing my beloved Brooklyn, I still enjoyed myself immensely as if being homesick was not an option. While the scope of my activities in London was limited to my teenage frame of reference, I took a lot of pleasure from just being there.

Being away from Brooklyn at the period in my life exposed me to experiences that just were not available in my city at the time. Most notably, I was able to go to raves in the clubs even though I was only 16 years old. Until this day, I believe my 6 foot height coupled with my virtual global VIP card, the US passport, goaded the bouncers at the clubs to ignore the fact I was not anywhere near legal. Up until that point, I had only attended a house party or two in America before going to England, however, the club experience for such a young first timer was incredibly unbelievable. It did not seem like real life, rather it was a living fantasy. Without a doubt, at that age, I would not have been able to gain entry into any club in New York City, so from that standpoint, I had already become used to comparing, contrasting and taking advantages of the differences between being at home and abroad, which I believe all travelers partake.

The pros and cons of London as compared to NYC were a constant on my mental chalkboard. No tourist sight, food item, vehicle or mode of transportation was exempt from my scrutiny. I do not remember which city won the competition, but I can say London had prettier, classier women while NYC had more basketball courts and cheaper sneakers. As a 16 year old kid, the sum of my young life and what I valued seemed to have come down to girls and basketball, as expected. Despite my relatively limited scope, the change in vantage point still gave me a broader, panoramic view of life. The highlight of my time there had to be watching the legendary Hip-Hop group; "The Fugees" perform at Brixton Academy. They performed a classic live version of "Killing Me Softly" that I still listen to from time to time.

In addition to the clothes and the music, I also fell in love with the British foods. Being that London was a melting pot full of places to go quite like my NYC, I found a job working a local chicken spot called *"King's Fried Chicken"* in order to pay for my exploratory expeditions around the city and my manic addiction to all things Hip-Hop. The restaurant was owned by two young Pakistani brothers and was like KFC mixed with East Indian curry style cuisine. A customer could purchase a 3 piece chicken meal with a biscuit or a mutton korma with roti bread. Eventually and quite naturally, I became quite fond of Indo-Pak foods while working there and, of course, I made a few friends from the people who patronized the establishment.

Outside of the restaurant, I came across an English snack dish that I thought to be their equivalent of French fries called "chips". Made from potatoes wedges, the chips were thicker than French fries and a lot tastier because the Brits seasoned the chips with salt and malt vinegar. For only ninety pence(a little over a dollar), I was able to have a tasty, fulfilling treat to hold me over until dinner was served. I had also come across a famous British drink made from black currants called Ribena, which was very different from anything I had ever tried up until that point. As it seemed, in Britain, it was common to buy concentrated syrup then add water to suit a person's own taste. Ribena was the first and the best concentrated drink or "cordial", I had ever tasted. While Ribena was my absolute favorite drink, the apple sodas in Britain were quite the treat as well. From the foods to the fashions to the down to earth people, I loved every bit of living in London. Moreover, until this day, I still have an affinity for the popular British drink made from concentrated black currant juice named Ribena.

I have also had the pleasure of traveling throughout a large part of America while touring as an independent Hip-Hop artist during my mid-twenties. The overall experience of witnessing how others live in different environments outside of NYC and the East Coast drastically altered my view of life and the world, as I knew it to be. The heartwarming experience of observing the similarities shared with people from different parts of the country or world warms the heart. There were people whose environments were the polar opposites of my own, but incredibly, we had shared common traits. It was also quite uplifting and awe-inspiring to witness the vast differences up close.

Today, as I pen these words from a small city high atop of a mountain in Saudi Arabia called Abha, I reflect on my experiences in every place that was not on the corner of Nostrand Avenue and Monroe Street where I was a fixture for a period of my life. Seeing the hippies in Lawrence, Kansas play banjoes in front on their Volkswagen van for spare change tickled me just as much as watching middle-aged men play spades on the streets of Madinah, Saudi Arabia. Even more amusing was watching the unlicensed vendors, aka the hustlers, of Madinah clear the block when the young boys who acted as the lookouts signaled that the police were approaching.

Its experiences like these that remind me how much people are the same despite cultural differences. Thinking back to John-John's unrelenting encouragement to travel, I remember asking him, "Why?" I now know why. The reason why I was encouraged to travel is blatantly obvious to me today. The reason is so profound and dynamic that I do not want to articulate it for fear that my feeble vocabulary would not be able to convey the whole of the benefits. All I can say is go see for yourself.

Unfortunately, I don't think many readers from my own community will take heed to this advice because the reality is most people from my culture do not travel the world save for a few trendy party and vacation destinations. I have had numerous conversations with various people who would much rather dress fancy in the same place they grew up in than hop on a plane then go to a place they've never been. And of course, I am referring to the majority of my peers from the Hip-Hop generation. A respected elder once told me that we wear airfare on our backs and parade around our hoods with the same monies that could be used for an experience of a lifetime. Regrettably, a lack of perception greatly limits our aspirations to the extent that many of us do not know the world is bigger than where we are from, what we know and what we are used to. I can remember days and nights spent on the corner with people who, like myself at that time, thought a 45-minute train ride to the Bronx, a different section of NYC, was a "journey". If a person thinks that 45 minutes on train is a long time then 12 hours on a plane is beyond his realm of comprehension. The result is that this person's world is as limited as the Earth is vast. Do not be that person.

Purchase a ticket then go then; after you go, observe then take in as much as you could. Do not be afraid to do something that you would not have normally done at home.

Please do not take my words as an encouragement to act like a hedonist, lustful savage while traveling, but rather as a push to try something new that people do not do where you are from. Maybe you will like sharing a dinner with strangers from a platter where everyone eats with their hands. On the other hand, maybe you will not. The point here is to try something new.

Obviously, I feel very strongly about this advice, especially if you are from the same type of environment that bred me. If by chance, you are from the other, better side of the tracks, the advice is the same. The benefits of seeing more will allow the traveler to be more.

"To be more what? More what"

The benefit of seeing more will allow the traveler to, hopefully, be more well rounded and tolerant towards the differences of others. Also, the traveler would be exposed to all sorts of cool stuff making him able to return home with a bunch of cool stories. Does this make sense?

For your benefit, I sincerely hope it does. Enjoy your travels and do not forget to take pictures. A wise man once told me that traveling is the only thing that you can buy that makes you richer. This wealth is not in a sense of material items but a richness of self. After crossing an ocean then nestling atop an 8000 feet mountain, I would definitely be more than inclined to concur.

The "N" Word

In 2008, I made my first trip to the Saudi Arabia for spiritual reasons. To put it bluntly, I left the Big Apple in order to get my mind right. The pace and overall environment of Gotham became extremely overwhelming, so I made my way to Mecca and Madinah, the two holy Islamic cities, for some introspection. I had also wanted to visit my mother and sisters who had lived in Saudi Arabia for close to 10 years at that time.

While there for my visit I initially donned my normal attire, which was always was something fresh off a rack in New York City's trendiest fashion neighborhood, Soho, yet in still, accentuated by an authentic Brooklyn demeanor. On my feet, I wore an exclusive pair of Adidas because the brand with three stripes were the only sneakers that did not make my size 13 feet look like the huge feet they are. My jeans, they were also pretty dope, but subtle and nondescript without any large markings or logos. I do not exactly remember the t-shirt, but I have always purchased cool tees to complete my ensembles. My outfit, hip-hop street wear, made it very easy for me to stand out like a sore thumb in the ultra-conservative holy city.

As I made my sightseeing rounds through the conservative holy city of Madinah, the young dudes would give me the twice over. Usually, they would stare at my shoes and this was expected because the same thing always happened in NYC as well. Most of the gawkers would usually keep it moving without saying a word, but one night of the main commercial strip, Sultanah Road, a young Saudi man struck up a conversation. His English was choppy, but I understood him well.

You American, saah? *Saah is short for Saheeh, which translates to "true" in English.*

I responded, "Na'am". *Arabic for yes.*

The white Arab teenager, a wiry thin 5'10, was obviously excited to meet me. He smiled from ear to ear while shaking my hand and smiling even more. His outfit was similar to my own in style but not in quality. The clothing was the typical knock-off merchandise tourists flock to the Wholesale District in Manhattan to buy. No judgment is passed because I have seen native New Yorkers with similar gear. However, as his eyes lit up he said five words that literally left me stuck on stupid. With a stoned cement confidence he said to me,

"Look. (Gesturing to his clothes) I'm nigga, I'm nigga."

I was completely at a loss for words because the dude literally went out of his way to tell me that he is a nigga and, furthermore, he seemed to be looking for some sort of validation. By then, I had traveled enough to know I should be prepared for encountering the unexpected and unimaginable. Even with that said; the young Saudi still managed to throw the craziest of curve balls. When I returned to the States after that initial visit, I told my people about the Arab teenager who told proudly declared to me, *"I'm nigga, I'm nigga"* and their responses were usually like my own; one of complete disbelief and bewilderment. Years later, I still shake my head in confusion when reflecting on that weird night. Wow.

SCENE II

Almost 3 years after I was blown away by the Arab kid proudly claiming to be a nigga, I was no longer a visitor, but a full-fledged expat with almost a year under my belt working as an English teacher to mostly well-off Saudi college kids in a small city called Abha in Southern Saudi Arabia. In my efforts to go the extra mile with my students, I gave out Blackberry instant messenger pin along with my email address. I figured they would hit me up whenever they needed help with English grammar or practice with conversation. This was my way of going the extra mile with the students in order to aid them as best I could.

One day during a class break I went about my normal social media routine, I switched my profile picture to the 22-year-old block hugging' Hamza or Humz, as I was called back then. The switch had no real reason other than I wanted a different profile avatar. In the new profile picture, I was wearing a tee with an image of Angela Davis wearing her divine afro in its full splendor. I also wore a red, black, and green headband as well as my customary Adidas sneakers. Essentially, I was rocking my normal, Hip-Hop urban attire. My students, up until that point, had only seen me wear bland tan Dockers and a basic blue Polo button-up. In effect, I was looking like a mail-room worker in corporate America or like a boring teacher.

So, during my class I received a BBM text from one of the sharper students shortly after I switched to the new picture.

The text read, "Cool Pic." Nigga! *smiley face*

More curious than shocked or offended I replied, "Nigga? What's that?"

Student replies: Nigga, like Hip-Hop dancer. Did you dance Hip-Hop?

Okay, so now I had a clear definition of nigga from the local youth who were undoubtedly exposed to American Hip-Hop culture probably by way of the internet. Again, I was not offended or shocked, but I wanted to have a better understanding of the college-aged students I was teaching. To his question I responded in the negative, as I was never a dancer but rather I was a rapper, then towards the end of the class I showed the guys some YouTube footage of me when I was an aspiring rapper. They all smiled emphatically as they had just found out that their new English teacher was actually a real American "nigga".

In the following weeks, some of the students would play different Hip-Hop songs on their phones then ask me if I knew the song or could translate the lyrics into simpler understandable English without the slang. One had the foolish nerve to ask me if I was familiar with the infamous Biggie & Tupac freestyle that is almost a mandatory knowledge for any Brooklyn resident from that era of New York City hip-hop. Needless to say, some of the Saudi youth have made good use of the internet by becoming familiar with two of the culture's biggest icons. I guess broadening one's own cultural scope just happens to be the human thing to do.

To be continued

The Prettiest Pearl

In 2008, during my first stay in the Kingdom of Saudi Arabia, I observed up close a struggle far more severe than anything I had ever encountered in the States. This trial was not my own, rather it was the struggle of many of the laborers working in the Kingdom. One day while I was leaving the local mosque after the pre-dawn prayer, a migrant worker from Sri Lanka named Armanallah invited me to his home for tea. Honestly, I did not want to go because it was so early in the morning and I wanted to go back to sleep, but I eventually obliged in accepting his humble invitation. One of the many Islamic customs I was made aware of involved accepting invitations, so with that in mind I went back to his home with him. At the time, I was unaware, but drinking tea in Armanallah's home would forever alter my life changing how I viewed things.

Armanallah was a short older man with a graying beard standing at around 5'7 with a rotund potbelly. His calm brown eyes were the perfect complement to his gentle handshakes. We walked for 3 minutes until we reached the front of a 4-story apartment with a marble façade, like all the others in that section our neighborhood. Armanallah worked at the building as the *haris*, which is the equivalent of a superintendent. His job was to clean the building and complete other handyman-like duties. Following his lead, we eventually stopped at a large iron door leading to an alleyway between his building and the building next door. Inside of the alley stood was what I believed to have been a shed. Armanallah walked to the door of the shed, unlocked it and then he said, *Tafaddal*, meaning, "welcome or enter". The shed was his home.

I was in sheer shock at his living quarters, but I tried hard to not let the surprise show on my face because doing such would have been extremely rude of me as his guest. His home looked almost like a prison cell in size. The walls were literally the cemented walls of the two buildings he lived in between. The roof was a thin sheet of plywood. His simple furnishings consisted merely of a twin-sized bed wedged horizontally between the two cement walls. There was also a medium sized refrigerator and a propane tank connected to single eye, which he used for cooking. The most telling appliance was an old-fashioned three speed, oscillating desk fan drilled to the wall directly over his bed. The meek fan stood out to me because the Madinah heat is a brutally dry easily reaching 115 degrees Fahrenheit in the summer months. Just as a cup of water is not enough to stop a large fire, his fan was no match for the city where the summer breezes feel like a hot blow dryer on the most sensitive parts of the ear. Those simple possessions were all that could fit inside his humble abode.

If a picture is worth a thousand words, then the live sight of Armanallah's home was undoubtedly the equivalent to the combined lexicons of every spoken language on Earth. When I looked into his home, I was so overwhelmed that I wanted to cry. As we stepped inside, he requested that I sit on his tiny bed while he prepared a cup of tea on the makeshift stove and retrieved a few dates from his refrigerator. He began to tell me about his family in Sri Lanka, his wife and his 3 daughters, all of whom his toil as a superintendent supports. His gentle eyes lit up as he proudly informed me two of his three daughters were married and going to college. He was also elated that he and his wife were able to perform the ritual Islamic rites of the *Hajj* pilgrimage, which is something people from poorer countries ,like Sri Lanka, save up a lifetime for. As we sipped on the tea and ate dates, I saw a hardworking family man, like myself, but he was in a position that I could never fathom.

After I had finished the first cup of tea, he offered me another cup. Then after we exhausted his dates, he offered me cookies. The cookies were stale, but I could not bring myself to reject his offering for fear of offending him. Honestly, the degree of poverty I was experiencing made me quite self-conscious about my own standards. How dare I turn down cookie even though it was stale even it was clear this poor man was graciously offering all that he could. I was instantly humbled. Sitting on his bed, while he sat on his floor I had begun to see something foreign to my eyes. Before me, there sat a poor man who offered me what seemed to be everything, while it was obvious he had nothing according to my American standards. Never in my life had I come across a person with nothing who was so giving. I was even more surprised by his demeanor and the content calm he projected. I asked myself, "How can a person so poor be so content and at peace with his situation?" At the time, I just could not understand it. Perhaps, being socialized with American culture obstructed me from grasping the secret to his calm.

While speaking with him, I saw a beauty as dynamic as anything I had witnessed prior to our talk. The beauty was so immense that it caused me to feel as if I did not have sight before I laid eyes on him. Armanallah radiated patience, gratitude, and generosity. I was totally in awe. Shortly thereafter, I had to excuse myself from his humble home; I needed a long walk to take in everything in. To me, it seemed I had just shared tea with the richest poor man in the world.

In retrospect, Armanallah taught me something about myself that had my mirror shown me, I would have surely smashed it to pieces. He inadvertently taught me about the ugliness of my own ingratitude and impatience with life. The lesson was one of perception, but it was broken into two aspects: attitude and gratitude. From his demeanor, then by witnessing his lifestyle, his patience was evident. Being able to carry his self with humble dignity during an extremely dire situation spoke volumes on his character. For instance, the building he worked in contained not just a marble and granite exterior, but the floors and the walls of the interior were also built with the creamy, shiny stones. This is how the majority of modern Saudi apartment buildings are furnished. If he were from those type of people with a half-empty, sour grape mentality, he would have undoubtedly looked at his situation in a negative light. That negative outlook would have surely affected the manner in which he carried out his goal. In fact, an attitude void of patience could have seriously jeopardized his family's lone source of income. So, how was he able to ignore the luxury of his workplace and focus solely on turning his relative squalor into his own personal castle? After giving myself some time, I finally reached a conclusion. Simultaneously, a beautiful pearl appeared in my right hand.

This pearl I pray to cherish for as long as my heart beats and my lungs have air is none other than gratitude. Being the humble guest of an even humbler man, bathed me in gratitude, the likes of which I did not know was possible. It became clear and evident to me that he could look at me as being fortunate, dare I say rich. I always knew "poverty was relative", but meeting Armanallah cemented what was once a thought inspired by a common saying into a firm clear reality. To further put things into context, at the time when I made the trip to Saudi Arabia I was living in a rough section of Brooklyn and my rented room was far from the snazziest pad. From time to time during that period, I had let ungratefulness get the best of me, ignorant to the fact there was someone who would see a mansion in my meager rented room. Looking at the nicer homes in my neighborhood blinded me from thinking about the places on Earth where "homes" are without running water and air conditioning. As the change in paradigm manifested itself, a single tear fell from my eyes. Soon after, one tear turned into a steady stream. Shame can be painful and verily I was ashamed of my attitude lacking of gratitude. How could I have been so blind in not acknowledging the smallest of fortunes bestowed on me? How could I?

I value this lesson of gratitude because from it, my life has gained more meaning and a greater depth. Changing the way I see the world around me has transported me to a new world and I am not afraid to admit this. It can be quite easy to get carried away focusing on the things I do not have, but valuing what I do have has made me feel more tranquil. I will never forget having tea with the richest poor man in the world, just as I will never forget to be grateful for every experience. Of course, I would love to step into the shoes of a man with great wealth, but I must never forget true wealth comes with valuing what one already possesses. This pearl of wisdom I owe solely to Armanallah.

In Saudi Arabia, it is a common practice to hire migrant workers from extremely poor countries as laborers. Some of these laborers leave their families for long periods to earn about $200 a month in. As we all know, poverty is relative. Now, please imagine the level of poverty in a country where a person would eagerly leave his/her family for the majority of the year for only $200USD monthly while working 6 days a week. What are the conditions in the poor neighborhoods of Sri Lanka, Indonesia, India, and other "developing" countries? Witnessing the men who have left their families reminds me of how fortunate I am to see the family I wake up early to provide for, every night. I have long been an admirer of the average immigrant's work ethic, but these migrant workers inspire me to new levels. Whenever I greet one of the many migrant throughout my day, they are always polite and welcoming. It is my goal to adopt their attitude of gratitude, in order to appreciate and value life as it should be valued.

Gratitude, the prettiest pearl

The N Word Yet Again

Still in the first semester of English courses in Abha, I befriended a very kind student named Muhammad Ali. Muhammad, as one can imagine, is an extremely popular name in Saudi Arabia. In fact, Muhammad is actually the most popular name in the entire world, but back to the story. Muhammad was in the English prep program as prerequisite for him to pursue his Masters in Business. He stood out to me because he was one of the few students who were religious. He was not preachy or anything like that, but his demeanor let me know he was religious and not into Western culture at all, so I befriended him. We would drink tea after class while I practiced my Arabic with him while simultaneously while he practiced his English on me.

Eventually, Muhammad invited me to his home for a dinner in honor of his elderly father, who had just been released from the hospital due to heart issues. It was my first time being the guest of honor in a Saudi home and I enjoyed the experience immensely. I practically met all of his male family members from his father to his uncles to his brothers and his cousins. His younger brother, Ahmad, had recently returned from an English program in Canada and was preparing to go to Boston for medical school. Ahmad and I spoke for a bit about the States, music, and the regular stuff an expatriate discusses with the locals. Then Ahmad made a request about a subject he was certain I knew about.

"Tell me about nigga. I want to know how to use it."

Of course, I obliged, but at first I wanted to know what how he defined the word. According to his understanding, a nigga was a person who was into Hip-Hop, but he most certainly heard that some people, particularly Blacks, do not like that word being used by other ethnicities. His definition mirrored the one my student gave me a few weeks prior. Once I saw what page he was on, I briefly gave him the rundown on the word, its origins; the initial intended use as well as the connotation of how it is currently used in Hip-Hop music, which is how he first heard the "N" word.

In a nutshell, I explained to him that the generations before me had negative feelings about the word because of the historical context. Then I told him that the current Hip-Hop generation is a little bit more lax with restrictions on other races using the N word, but to be on the safe side he should not use the word when he reaches America. This was my advice for him because I did not want him blurting out "Nigga" in an off-key context then getting beat up by someone. He understood my words then we both agreed that any word directed in a derogatory manner towards a person could be offensive, but words that are considered a slur to some will more than likely offend.

That was my third encounter with the nigga word in the Kingdom of Saudi Arabia and each time I gained more of an understanding about the Saudi youth, the widespread influence Hip-Hop culture and how they intersect. As expected, some of the Saudi youth have embraced the Hip-Hop culture through fashion and music. Unbelievably,

Akon is really popular with the youth in Saudi. It is also quite obvious that embracing Hip-Hop culture is the "cool-thing" to do for those youth, and there's nothing cooler than to be "the nigga" or a nigga".

Interesting, right?

Dinner at Muhammad's

There were a few exploits that I had on my "submersion in a foreign culture bucket list", but none was more endearing than being able to first-hand experience the legendary hospitality of the Arabs. The stories I have heard from others about being the guest of honor in a traditional Arab home seemed too good to be true. A companion of mine relayed to me his experience in complementing a piece of art only to be given the art he admired directly off the wall. Bashfully he declined as the host insisted on him leaving the home with the artwork. Finally, he graciously accepted the artwork he was so enamored with. Such are the tales of Arab hospitality that are based on traditions stretching back well over a millennia.

Hearing these tales made me eager to experience being a guest of honor and, quite honestly, who would not want experience that high level of selfless generosity and hospitality. One of the moments I had been waiting for came when a student named Muhammad invited me to his family's home to celebrate his father, the family's eldest patriarch, returning home from a stay in the hospital due to a heart condition. In honor of such a joyous event, the family threw him a dinner and by custom, a lamb or two were slaughtered.

Muhammad and I had spent time together practicing each of our respective target languages, his was English and mine was Arabic, and also discussing minor details of Islam. He had actually graduated from a prestigious Islamic university, so I took full advantage by asking him various questions about the faith. Over tea, we conversed getting to know one another. His gentle demeanor and soft-spoken nature made him one of my favorite students and friends during my time in his mountainous city of Abha. After a number of great conversations over tea coupled with an event to invite me to, the opportunity was presented to me during class evening. Initially, I had plans but I quickly canceled those plans because it was an opportunity I could not pass up.

Anxiously I left with Muhammad directly after class had ended. Prior to going to his parent's home, he made a few stop in the area, one of which was a stop at the mosque in his neighborhood or village as he called. At the mosque, I met a few of his cousins, all of whom were very welcoming and friendly to me. After we participated in the prayer coinciding with sunset we headed over to his parent's home which was a short ride away. A short dirt road led us directly to a large3 story villa surrounded by a huge cement wall. Directly next to the villa was an old two story clay and mud antique Arab home, which looked as if it was directly out of an exhibit at New York's Museum of Natural History. I was told, by Muhammad, that the home belong to his grandparents and was not demolished in order to maintain tradition. At the moment, I was unaware how firmly his family held onto to tradition but in the coming hours, it was made clear to me.

We entered the home of Muhammad's parents through a side entrance then I was led to a corridor housing sinks in the hallway. In tradition Arab homes sinks used to the ritual ablution needed to make the daily prayers can be found in hallways, foyers, and odd places one would not find a sink in regular Western homes. In following Muhammad, I slid off my shoes then washed my hands just as he did. We then entered a large sitting room with wall-to-wall couches on every wall and seated in the corner immediately viewable upon entering the room was an elderly man eating dates talking with a much younger man.

Muhammad took me in the direction of the old man, who happened to be his father, in order to greet him and the man he was talking to, the first-born son. There were maybe four other people sitting around the room scattered about so I took the nearest seat to me because I was nervous in such an unfamiliar environment. Also, I didn't want to offend anyone with my ignorance of the customs of the home. The older man observed my anxiousness then gestured for me to sit directly next to him on the opposite side of his eldest son. After sitting beside the patriarch of the dates were offered by Muhammad's father from which I ate a few just to accept his offering. Deliciously sweet and supple, I wanted to eat more of the dates, however, I was careful not to offend, so I only ate a few until my host gestured for me to eat more.

It was around this time other men began filing into the spacious sitting room; one by one, each of whom walked over directly to Muhammad's father then kissed his forehead as a show of respect. Young men and men in the same age range of the patriarch each kissed his forehead before shaking his hand. Such a beautiful show of respect made me smile each time it happened. As the room and couches began to fill the young boys of the family played their traditional role by serving dates and coffee to their elders. One boy was charged with walking around room offering dates from a fine stainless platter, while another boy followed behind him with a pot of fragrant Arab coffee. When each boy reached the patriarch, they kissed his right hand before kissing his forehead. The custom for the young boys was different from those who had reached the age of   maturity.

This continued for some time: men entering and greeting, young boys circling the room serving dates and coffee, Muhammad's father gesturing me to eat more and more dates until one of the boys made the announcement that dinner was ready to be served. We were all led to another where on the floor laid out were two very large platters of lamb and rice. The portions, still steaming, looked very large lying over the yellow rice speckled with raisins, almonds and spices. Surrounding the platters were grapes, bananas, and oranges along with bottles of spring water and cans of soda. Still unaware of the customs, I waited for someone to sit then I found a space of my own that was not next to the father only to learn the guest of honor at such occasions sits in between the father and the eldest son. For that, indeed, I felt honored, but it did not stop there. After we sat at the platter grabbing morsels of lambs along with handfuls of rice thus beginning the meal, the eldest son picked at the lamb, taking meat from certain sections. Each time he grabbed the morsel of meat from the section of choice cuts he then placed the meat directly in front of me almost as if to treat me to the best part of the lamb. Again, I was floored by such thoughtful and selfless hospitality. The meat was tender beyond belief blending perfect with the rice that was served.

Curiously, the young boys were not eating with us, so I had assumed they were eating their fill in another room similar to us. As we ate with our hands, the family members spoke amongst themselves telling jokes and enjoying the atmosphere until we had eaten more than enough then they began to eat from the fruit surrounded the two platters. Fruits in America are usually part of breakfast or a snack but never a side dish to a dinner, however different it was to me I follow suit eating from the grapes and bananas while washing them down with mouthfuls of spring water. Shortly thereafter, I noticed the men pick the bones from the two platters then placing them to the side. Perhaps "they are to removing them to feed the family pets", is what I thought to myself, but I was wrong. Once the bones had been removed from the platters, the men stood up to exit while the young boys filed in. Mistakenly I thought the young boys were eating in another room, however, they were waiting for the adult men to eat their fill, so they could partake in the feast afterwards in keeping in line with their customs. The men all returned to the large sitting room for tea and more conversation while the boys ate. After eating I was a lot more comfortable than when I first arrived, so I mingle a bit more with the English speaking family members. A few cups of tea and some jokes were told then everyone bid farewell going on about their affairs. Muhammad, of course, drove me home while asking me how I liked his family and the dinner in which I replied with praise and gratitude for both. At that moment, the full scope of what I had just witnessed and been a part of began to register.

Within these centuries old practices were familial exchanges unlike anything I had ever observed in my own country and culture. The honoring of the elder, both by the young boys as well as the adults who were other than the patriarch, in my humble opinion, served as symbolical way of maintaining the traditions of old. The servitude of the young towards the old seemingly instilled a reverence and respect for the elders thus forging a strength between generations; whereas, in America with each generation there is gap. The honoring of the guest, I believe, acts as a precursor to establishing ties outside of the family based on treating others how you would like to be treated. The sitting between the patriarch and the eldest son seemed to be show of the importance placed on the guest accepting the invitation.

Admittedly, I did not query Muhammad for an explanation of the significance of each of the customs displayed at dinner that night. He would have been more than delighted to explain everything in detail, but there was a great chance he was long removed from the reasoning behind each gesture, left solely to mimicking the customs for the sake of tradition. Whether there was a deeper significance or not, each of the gestures towards me and amongst themselves made the night one that will live with me for all of my days.

My amateur analysis merely adds to my own experience, perhaps, romanticizing mundane tasks into something much more significant and that I can accept. In any case, the night I spent at Muhammad's childhood home for dinner was as epic of a travel experience that I have had to date far exceeding all expectations I had of the legendary hospitality of the Arabs. For not only did I experience graciousness firsthand, but I had also witnesses it displayed in multitudes beyond my scope of familiarity.

American Me

We, the American folk, are a people of alphas. Americans believe we have the best chunk of land on the entire Earth with the best governing system and all the works to come with it. America is the most desirable place on Earth to live and visit, isn't it? I, for one, always thought so if only due to hearing the sentiment oft repeated throughout my years. Is there any truth to it? I cannot quite answer that but a better question would be: Is there any way to prove this? Since the former is subjective, the latter question has to be answered in the negative. If this is agreed upon, then the entire "America is the greatest country on Earth" thing is hogwash, a mere nationalist slogan void of any factual claim. Despite this many Americans assume this as an absolute truth then go on to adopt the air of entitlement along with the infinite and infallible wisdom that erroneously comes with it, or so we think.

While in America surrounded, in majority, by Americans I was quite unaware of my own American ways. The reason this is simple: it is difficult to see one's own height in a room full of people standing at the same height. There were times, while in America when I briefly hung around the pocket communities of immigrants observing and, at times, participating in their cultural doings. It was only during those times when I felt awkwardly American. It was only when I was surrounded with people from other cultures was I able to identify some of our own American ways, one of which is the attitude that our way is just better, by default. The most visible example of this on a large scale can be found when the American military invades countries to, among other reasons; establish a democracy, which in modern times is known as the American way of governing. We are apt to enter into a person's home (land) then revamp the way things are done there because "our way is just better". This was made even clearer to me while working as an English instructor at a small business college in Abha, Saudi Arabia.

Shortly after the start of the academic year, which coincided with my 10th month abroad, my immediate supervisor and head of my department approached me with what seemed to be a career advancing opportunity. I was offered a promotion from instructor to an administrator. Barely a semester into moonlighting as a TEFL (Teaching English as a Foreign Language) instructor, I was on my way to becoming Brooklyn's Rosetta Stone or so I thought. The promotion called for me to spend less time in the classroom and more time in the office handling the administrative affairs of the English department. It sounded good on the surface, but I graciously turned down the promotion even though it seemed like a very good opportunity for advancement. Since that was my first time ever teaching, I sought out a lot of advice prior to securing employment from other American and British expatriates in KSA on everything from teaching English as a second language as well as how to deal with the locals on a professional level.

As with any workplace, having a good understanding of the politics is essential to, at the very least, keeping one's job. My friends that have been in Kingdom for some time told me that some of the locals have a habit of passing off work responsibilities to others, usually foreigners. If by chance the employee fumbled the ball he would, of course, be terminated. If the tasks were handled accordingly the person who shirked off his responsibilities would, of course, take the credit. Knowing this "great opportunity" seemingly expedited a trip to the firing squad known as the Human Resources department or add work with no extra compensation, I turned the promotion down while my coworkers, most of whom were not privy to the office politics in Saudi Arabia, looked at me as if I was the fool.

One such coworker, a fellow Black American, was then offered the same great position to which he eagerly accepted despite my warnings about how things were likely to transpire. In the following weeks, as the new administrative coordinator he revamped the entire English program by instituting a myriad of new policies. The other teachers and I quickly grew tired of the newly mandated bi-weekly meetings along with the numerous other tweaks, which really seemed to be a show of power rather than anything significant. Eventually the students also became quite weary of the change in culture as well.

During that period in Saudi Arabia, schooling was far different than in the United States from the standpoint that schools were looked at as businesses with the students being the customers, which is the opposite of what I was used to in America. Furthermore, they have adopted the "Customer is always right" ethos, which lead to quite the problem when a student was not pleased with his grade or was not able to take an exam due to excessive absences, a policy that was implemented and strictly enforced by the new administrative coordinator.

The students, all of whom received a monthly stipend from the government to attend the courses, were angry because a failing grade in the English program would bar them from advancing thus putting a stop to the allowance they received to study. Honestly, by gauging the level of involvement and effort at this particular school I would say the majority of students were there just to get a monthly check. The culture was not one were academic achievements were made to be valued. As one very wealthy student told me, "My grandfather is from Abha and my grandchildren will be from Abha. So, I don't need English." Even though a student like this was guaranteed to miss more than half of the course and fail, he would still bring his father in to argue his failing grade. After some tough talk then, for instance, reminding the Dean that their families have known each other for generations, the failing grade would become a passing grade and the student would advance to the next level even if his English skills were less than stellar. Again, I was made aware of the culture long before I set foot inside of the classroom which in turn allowed me to navigate the waters with more tact than what would have been expected of a first time teacher in that foreign country.

The coworker who took the position could have used the same advice I was given. In fact, I relayed to him what was told to me just to inform him, but did not take heed. He must have been thinking I was trying to sabotage his promotion, but in reality, I did not want to see him led to the slaughterhouse. Well, as fate would have it 3 months into his regime he was suddenly removed from his position as administrative coordinator then ultimately let go completely. His error was being too American in a foreign land.

Attempting to change the currents of the ocean is examining the limits of futility. Moreover, trying to change the culture in which you are a foreigner is, in fact, trying to change the currents. I understood this but my colleague did not. Feeling the need to change the immediate environment to one that is more suitable is not necessarily unique to Americans, rather I believe it applies to all people, yet in still my compatriots do have a way of putting our stamp on things. As America has industrialized the modern world, English has become the most preferred way of doing business hence the large demand for English teachers in

Saudi Arabia. Other places, such as Dubai and Abu Dhabi, have even adopted Western models of infrastructure, which is in stark contrast to the traditional way of doing things in the Gulf Coast. For example, the process needed to secure a visa in the United States is uniform throughout the entire country with little room illegal side dealings. An applicant fills out the necessary paperwork then awaits approval. It is as simple as that. However, in the Middle East the traditional way operates much differently in that there are intermediaries, who act as expeditors, personally walking the application papers through to a contact inside the visa office. This seemed to be the case in every branch of government services and, furthermore, by American standards the quality of the service at these municipal facilities left so much to be desired

Imagine running an errand to the Department of Motor Vehicles to renew your license. After waiting for your number to be called you approach the window to find the agent either does not know how to complete your common request or just sits there drinking tea while smoking a cigarette because he does not feel like doing any work. Both instances are how things were done in Saudi Arabia and many expatriates who have lived in the Kingdom can attest to this. Now, in the first instance what usually happens is you would be directed to another window or desk to aid in processing your request, i.e. a signature. Next, it is routine to be sent to yet another window for another signature then to another window for yet another signature. Daunting and exhausting, it most definitely is, yet this is how things were done in Saudi Arabia during my time, either it's a long drawn process or your paperwork gets stuck on the desk of someone who doesn't feel like working that day. Of course, this can all be avoided by paying an intermediary to have the papers processed for you.

Coming from a place where occurrences like those were unheard of, it was easy for me to say things were backwards there. That would have been me passing judgments on the Saudis using my American frame of reference. While passing judgments in this manner is natural, it is not fair to their culture and way of doing things. The Saudis have a manner of conducting business that seems to be acceptable and feasible in their culture and who am I, as a guest, to state it is wrong. That would have been very insensitive to their culture as well as quite arrogant; however, as a native of the best country on Earth doing such was like a reflex.

Unbeknownst to Americans, we have a reputation abroad that is not the most pleasant and I contend that much of it is rooted in our predisposition to think we are the best in everything. Knowing this, I had made an extra effort to not judge the customs of locals; rather I observed then sought to make sense out of what differed from my own. How does this work for them?" I asked myself constantly. This approach was introduced to me by way of the book "The 7 Habits of Highly Effective People" which stated a person must first seek to understand than to be understood. It was incumbent on me, as an immigrant in a foreign land, to strive towards understanding the local people and customs before anything else, including passing judgments, and I would like to think I became very proficient in the task. By doing such I was able to transcend my American attitude of global supremacy and appreciate Saudi culture a bit more thus improving the overall quality of my experience as an expat.

A prime example of this is what directly led to me being offered the administrative position mentioned earlier. The day before I was presented with the prospective promotion I was in a heated argument with my supervisor over wages and job responsibilities. I was told bluntly to leave if I did not like the wage, which was considerably less than what was originally agreed upon at hiring. I strongly replied that the wage was already determined and he could kiss my ass. The exchange between the two of us was, surprisingly, very loud and raucous. While arguing with the supervisor, my American colleagues urged me to chill out, but for very good reason I chose to take heed.

In my time observing the locals prior to taking the job as an English teacher, I noticed something: they were able to have big arguments then make up and become friends afterwards. Arguments that would have, in America, led to blows were ended in Saudi Arabia with a hug then a cup of tea as an olive branch of sorts. Knowing this, I confidently engaged in the type of argument with a superior that would have left me without a job if I had done the same in America. The very next day after our argument I was offered a promotion by the same supervisor who I had just berated then made up with. Strange, right?

As travelers and expatriates, we often compare the lands of our travels to our countries of origin and, again, this is a natural response. However, in order to fully appreciate the new culture we must resist that automated response to deem everything that differs from what we know to be normal as weird and just take it all in. This is how one submerses himself into a new culture and transcends that which was left behind.

Surviving vs. Living - An Epiphany

Surviving to endure or live through (an affliction, adversity, misery, etc.)

I know about surviving against the odds. My first foray into the life of surviving was prior to adulthood. Due to circumstances, I was forced to learn how to sustain myself while navigating the trials of the inner city of Brooklyn. The constant barrage of difficulties thrown at me from every possible angle required the agility of a cheetah and the fortitude of a mountain. This was life as I knew it and shortly after this realization, I began to accept this type of existence. I was a firefighter, of sorts, from a standpoint where it seemed like my all was dedicated to putting out fires all around me, so I would not be burned like so many others who have walked down my road. Fires such as scrambling to pay rent and bills only to do it over and over again month after month with no relief lest I was open to living in a shelter.

Some of these fires were from my hands like misappropriating my funds while others were just what life necessitated. Regardless of the causes, my life was one difficulty after another. "This can't be life", is what I told myself unable to fully accept the common occurrences that never allowed me to thrive. All the while, something deep within stood in direct opposition to accepting survival mode. While I soon became quite adept at surviving, I knew there had to be more to life, another way. There had to be a lifestyle where rent and food was not the monthly goliaths I had to battle with. I wondered if my necessities were such an uphill battle then how I could possibly move myself into a space where I could take hold of the all the extras life had to offer. Honestly, I could not see a light at the end of the tunnel.

Common sense told me, in order to ascend out my situation I would have to save money, but the reality that is living in a New York City did not allow me to save anything. Every month I had a knife to my neck, so to speak. This means that I was very close to an extremely dire situation and this was the norm. Like clockwork, the days just prior to payday were quite the struggle. With the monies from the last pay period spent, I normally had to make do without for a few days until the next pay period. At the time, I was not making a huge sum, so I thought, "It's only like this because I my money is low". However, I noticed friends who made money more than myself experiencing the same trials. Then when I finally began to make better money, I was still in this familiar situation. I just could not figure out why. To this day, I only have a vague idea as to why this phenomenon exists, but the final result is crystal clear to me. Survival is usually all we know and if it is a struggle to clutch the bare minimum needed to keep alive, and then the odds of us learning what it is to live are slim to none.

Living - active or thriving; vigorous; strong

This is the definition for living that I have adopted because this definition calls for more than:

Living- having life; being alive; not dead

My definition of choice is also more than

Living - in actual existence or use; extant

Strong, active, vigorous are how I would like to lead my life, therefore you should understand why this is the definition I cling too dearly. The connotation of a vigorous life differs greatly from just having life or to be in existence. The active life is a life that is full of, life. While the life of survival is, the life that is always in searches of maintaining or holding on to life. In the old neighborhood, we had a term, "*Livin'*". I will define living by its antonym, or by what opposes. Livin', as those in my Hip-Hop culture know it to mean, is simply, not struggling. Livin' is not worrying about the necessities like food, clothing, shelter and safety. Livin' is a life void of an excessive amount of concerns, the worries and fears that are so constant that a person rarely if ever has a chance to breathe easy. This is living. Living is a life where the bare necessities have been met.

By the Grace of God, I am currently in a space where I am free from the worries of my younger years. I have survived many perilous situations, but today I am living. Ten years ago, I was ignorant to what it meant to be living and this was due to, not only my surroundings, but also, my lack of life experience. This state is where I will strive to be for as long as I have life because this is life, lived to the fullest extent. Gone are the days were my physical safety was in constant danger. Gone are the days of survival. While the future lies in God's Hands, I will use the same resourcefulness and diligence I used to pull me from a life a survival. Therefore, I guess I am still surviving, but this form of survival is about holding on to what allows me to thrive and this is how life should be lived.

New Eyes

This was originally a blog entry posted during my second year in Saudi Arabia. In revisiting this piece, after my return to the States, with new eyes it seems spacey and weird, almost foreign to me. Almost 2 years since coming home to the rat race known as life in NYC the concept of "living" is now distant as I am once again in survival mode. Since I left the cost of living has risen over 20% and rents are through the roof in my Brooklyn. Everything simply costs more; everything.

In reconnecting with my friends and associates, I heard stories of the struggle that is living in NYC; the same lifestyle I jumped across an ocean to avoid was still swallowing everyone whole. Almost everyone was feeling the squeeze of what is becoming a city for the wealthy. More and more people are renting out rooms and picking up side hustles to help cover monthly expenses. Money is what is on everyone's mind and rightfully so. Everyone is on a 29-day grind to keep a roof over their heads and, with new eyes, it became overwhelmingly obvious.

During one of my first morning commute on the subway, after returning, I entered a train car then proceeded to find a seat. After getting comfortable in my seat, I looked around the car just to be aware of my surrounding because it is, after all, New York City. What I saw were glum faces and tired eyes on almost everyone regardless of gender, race and age. To me, it seemed a lot deeper than being weary from lack of rest. Put off by the stone expressions and cold eyes, I felt as if I was riding to a wake or some over somber inducing event. This is what surviving in the Big Apple does to people.

This culture of survival is an environment burdened with stress that devours, eating away at happiness leaving most to exude from their faces a type of tired that is more than physical. Prior to crossing, the ocean I had an inkling that something was not right in my native environment, however my new eyes have turned that inkling into certainty. Indeed, something is not right.

In life, of course, the bills have to be paid and in order to accomplish this one must go out and earn by way of working. This is unavoidable; however, to be inundated constantly with the burden of bills is no way to experience the beauty of life. One needs time and a clear mind to fully enjoy life and unfortunately, when in survival mode those things are difficult to attain.

As I currently work myself out of survival mode yet again, I wonder if others have had this same epiphany. Being able to experience something other than survival mode gave me an insight I could not find prior to leaving America. At that time, I was in a very good position financially, but it is still different than the lifestyle I was afforded while teaching English in the Middle East, where I was able to cover the year's expenses with 3 months of salary. I was, most definitely, living. Moving forward, I now know how the light at the end of the tunnel feels like and I need that comfort back in my life. In fact, I wish it on all who are on the hamster wheel known as surviving.

Safety Concerns

Okay, I can admit that a young Black male of the Hip-Hop generation voluntarily relocating than submersing into Middle Eastern culture is a quite peculiar and an interesting tale. If I was ignorant to this, my friends definitely made me aware to the fact to the compelling nature of my journey shortly after I made the big jump. By way of my social media pages, they peppered me with loads of questions about living in Saudi Arabia and Kuwait. There were many questions that were frequently posed to me, but the one, which I heard most often pertained to the perceived safety concerns they thought I put myself in the middle of.

Is it safe out there?

This question is very telling because it is indicative of the media's ability to dictate narratives to an unassuming public. The average American thinks every country in Persian Gulf is a war-zone. Countries such as Saudi

Arabia, Kuwait, Jordan and basically every other Arab country are perceived to be unsafe by public opinion. While some countries with unstable governments are prone to internal strife, the presumption that Saudi Arabia, for instance, is not safe is the furthest thing from reality. I, a Black American, felt safer in the Middle East than I have ever felt in my own country, which I hate to admit, however I am obligated by the truth. The level of comfort experienced in Saudi Arabia was at such a degree I rarely left home with my keys nor did I lock my door at night even with my family inside my home. This was something I could never do in New York City unless I content with returning home to an empty abode.

While the safety concerns seem legitimate on the surface, they are somewhat baffling considering the range of crime prevalent in the United States. Violence stemming from drugs and gangs has affected almost every community in America with varying levels. Those two plagues are not prevalent in the countries I lived in nor do they have unusually high rate of death by police officers which

America leads all industrialized countries in. Safety from crime was not a concern during my time in those countries. I can understand concern stemming from people who must lock the doors to their homes, cars, and be vigilant at all times. That lifestyle where survival is the primary focus lends to constantly gauging one's own safety.

While in the Middle East I have never felt safer, however, it must be noted I stayed out of countries with unstable governments such as Egypt, Iran, Syria, Yemen and all the other places making news for internal turmoil. Violence was never a concern for me and neither was theft. One late night while eating at local McDonald's in Kuwait I absentmindedly left my phone at the restaurant then went home. The next morning I woke up only to be unable to locate my phone. After tearing up my place up, I thought back to the last place I remember having my phone, and surely, it was McDonald's. A long shot it was, but with a prayer, I proceeded to return to the fast food spot with the hopes that some may have seen the phone. Again, this was a wild guess, but it was all I had aside from purchasing new phone.

Upon entering the McDonald's, I went straight to the counter to request the manager. After explain my dilemma for 30 seconds he looked under the counter then pulled out my phones. He told me a customer brought the phone up to the counter shortly after I had left. As one could expect I was eternally grateful at the moral integrity of the person who found my phone and the staff who secured it until I returned. It pains me to say that something like this is unheard of America. Similarly, another situation involved a private English lesson I was conducting in a local Starbucks in Kuwait. My lesson coincided with the afternoon prayer time, so my student and I prepared ourselves to go to the prayer room inside of the mall. I automatically began to put my laptop inside of my briefcase when my student stopped then told me that doing such was not necessary. Being from a place where things are stolen within a blink of an eye, the idea of leaving my things unattended was unimaginable. My student and I proceed to go to the mall's prayer room where we spent about 20 minutes away from our unattended items. Upon returning to the Starbucks, our property was still there. As we can see, not only was I removed from the everyday violence, but I was also free from thieves and those who immediately seek to keep lost items to profit off those who are careless.

The normal concerns of the average New Yorker were just not present for me during my time abroad. The assumed concerns of extremist attacks or being kidnapped were also not a concern. There were safety concerns but not from the type Americans would normally think about. Remember, the Gulf countries are a different culture with an emphasis on different. Every land has dangers, but rarely are the dangers the same for two lands with differing terrains, climates, species, or in this case: cultures. Deaths caused by car accidents are extremely high in the countries of the Persian Gulf.

In Saudi Arabia, the driving was so reckless I was scared stiff to drive. Reckless as in high speed, last minute lane switches to the right from the far left lane without signaling in order to reach the exit on the highway. Or the more common left turns from the far right lane or vice versa at the intersections. The roads of that country were extremely dangerous. As one can imagine, traffic enforcement is very lax with there being no real penalty for speeding or reckless driving. Without those balances in place, the locals inadvertently play bumper cars with real cars. In addition, the youth have taken advantage of the lax traffic enforcement by racing and drifting on public streets.

Drifting is when the driver of a car speeds then jerks the wheels to the left and the right causing the car to skid around the road. Highly dangerous, some of these youth have become quite adept at handling the cars while drifting. Unfortunately, mistakes and crashes are bound to happen which ultimately resulted in me losing a handful of students. If I were teaching in Chicago's South Side, I would have presumably lost a student or two to gang violence, but in the Middle East the prevailing dangers are quite different. As always, the emphasis should be placed on the word: different.

I honestly wonder if other nationalities have the same concerns for safety that Americans have when travelling abroad. Understanding that America is generally crime ridden, it is totally understandable why safety is our main concern. Acknowledging this is also should also push my fellow Americans to examine the environment we live in. Perhaps, the greatest country on Earth has some things that need to be worked on just like all other nations do.

The Beheading (Journal Entry)

September 19th 2010.

The Holy City of Madinah, Kingdom of Saudi Arabia

I have been in the Kingdom for about 9 months now. I have endured the brutal Arabian summer and I am also pretty familiar with Islamic culture, so I do feel adjusted and acclimated to some extent. As expected, I am enjoying this place despite the mega slow pace of things and the weirdness of the native culture. Today started just like any other day with the predawn adhan, "call to prayer", signaling to the people in the neighborhood that it was time to offer the first of the five daily prayers to the Creator of the Heavens and Earth. I walked to one of the many houses of worship, "masjids", in my neighborhood then offered my prayer as usual. After prayer, I went on with my daily routine of studying until the sun had risen then I went back home for breakfast. At around 8:30 am, I received a phone call informing me that a public execution would be held shortly in the "town square".

Honestly, I jumped at the opportunity to witness this and, honestly, I was looking forward to it for some curious yet macabre reason. Despite my lifelong familiarity with Islam, I had never experienced this one aspect. Being a Muslim from The West where the Shariah is not applicable by the standards set by Shariah, there was no way I would have been able to see a beheading in the States. Most Americans do not know that Shariah can only be applied in Muslim countries. Misinformation stemming from the misunderstandings of misguided Muslim would have the public thinking otherwise. However, here I am in the Kingdom of Saudi Arabia where the Shariah is applied, so it is only right that I experience and observe as much of their culture as possible, an execution included.

After receiving the phone call, I immediately threw on my long white robe, or a *"thawb"* as it is called, then I headed to the place where the beheading was schedule to take place. The "town square" was actually the large parking lot of a government building and to my surprise; I was not the only spectator on hand for the event. Men of all ages were there patiently waiting to see the beheading, many of whom were locals who I presume have witnessed this before. Surrounding the perimeter of the parking lot were armed Saudi police officers standing at ease to act as crowd control. The time went on and more spectators crowded around the large parking lot. Some men even brought their young children there to witness the event.

After about an hour of standing under the merciless Arabian sun, a large procession of police vehicles entered the massive parking lot. There was also an ambulance, a few official unmarked government vehicles with groups of Saudis inside them, a fire truck, and the police van carrying the prisoner. At that time, I still did not know what the offense was, but it did not matter because I know people are not beheaded for stupidity, as would be the case in an extremist type of scenario. He had to have done something egregiously despicable then went through the local due process in order to receive this sentence.

So, the police cars were parked in a single file along one side of the lot while one police cruiser with a large bullhorn on the roof drove the center. From inside of the unmarked government cars exited a few regular looking people. There was an older male, an older female, and few other non-police looking people. "Okay, now the show is about the go down", I thought to myself as players started to emerge. The crowded packed itself as close to the barricade as possible because the middle of the parking lot was at least 300 feet away from cordoned off area. Standing at 6'4, I did not need to be directly on the barricade to get a bird's eye view, but the locals, most of whom were short men did.

After about 20 minutes, one of the officials placed a large cardboard in the center of the parking. There were maybe 15 different men in that vicinity, so I really could not tell who was who. I knew the prisoner was still in the police van but I could not identify the executioner at that point. After the cardboard was placed on the asphalt ground, the police van pulled up right beside it, and then the backdoor was opened by one of the men in the immediate area. Out stepped a man holding one of those old school doctor's bags, then I started to feel my heart thump through my chest, "It's going down, it's going down."

Shortness of breath followed and I was actually nervous. While I have witnessed senseless ghetto violence (shootings and deaths) from an early age, this was something very different. I cannot put my finger on why this was different but it was. Simultaneously, as the prisoner was removed from the police van, a police officer went the police car at the middle of the parking then got on the bullhorn. The prisoner, handcuffed with his hands behind his back, was taken from the patty wagon to the cardboard. He was then instructed to kneel down in a lotus position. By this time, the executioner was already on hand and a bowed sword was drawn. From a distance, I could tell the sword was extremely long. I am estimating it was probably 3 and half feet long. My anxiety over the ordeal did not allow me to see where the sword came from. To my recollection, none of the 15 men were carrying a sword prior to the prisoner's exit from the van. My vantage point was briefly obstructed when then police van pulled up to the spot.

At this time, the policeman with the bullhorn got on the loudspeaker. He started with a prayer then he said, all in Arabic, "The charges are four......" The executioner holding the bowed sword in his right hand said something to the prisoner as he knelt. Maybe it was a prayer, I do not know. He then guided the prisoner's head by placing his hand to the side of the prisoner's face almost as if to say, "This is the position you need to be in so I can take your head cleanly." It reminded me of the how a barber guides a person's face in order trim a beard. Then the executioner raised his sword and dropped it on the back of the prisoner's neck with one strong clean swipe. "Wow"

The prisoner's head dropped then rolled a few feet away while his body sat still, knelt over in the same position it was in when he took his last breath. "Wow"

Blood began to pour skirt and gush from his headless body as the executioner poured a bottle of water on his sword to clean the razor sharp blade. The show was over and the locals began to file out but I stood there in total shock, unable to move, trying to process what I had just witnessed.

"WOW "

A short time thereafter, the lifeless, headless body was laid down on the ground by one of the men on the scene. I asked my companion what were the charges, as I did not fully comprehend the address on the loudspeaker. I was told the man had become drunk then he broke into a home while the husband was at work. He then savagely beat and raped the woman of the household. My companion also informed me, the regular looking folk who exited the unmarked vehicles were from the family of the victim. A little while later after most of the blood exited the man's body, he was placed on a stretcher then his head was retrieved then placed on the stretcher as well. The body and detached head were then placed inside of the ambulance as I still stood with my legs seemingly rooted into the ground.

At I loss for words, I really do not know what to think however I cannot pass judgment on the execution for a few reasons. The first reason is the punishment is based on a divine law, according to Islam, that I have no right to object because I am not divine. Secondly, being a guest in a foreign culture who am I to comment on their culture and laws. Where I am from, peoples' lives are taken for positioning in the drug trade, "disrespect", greed, rage, and a myriad of other senseless reasons. In addition, the American justice system seems to be quite malleable when the defendant can afford quality legal representation or if race plays a role. Because of this, many crimes go unpunished and those who are punished are rarely rehabilitated or "corrected", as the name "correctional facility" implies. Shortly after my entry into the Kingdom, I can recall a case in NYC where an ex-con recently released from prison for rape, proceeded to rape an elderly woman his mother was the caretaker for. The pervert was not out of prison for an entire year before he raped a helpless old woman. While trying to Google the pertinent link for this blog, I could not find that incident but I did find quite a few more similarly disgusting cases throughout the states.

Would things be different if proven rapists and murders were beheaded in the States? I wholeheartedly believe so because as I write this entry at 2:30am, I hear the sounds of children, as young as 6 years old, playing in the streets below me. The safety that is evident in their leisurely activities is one of the main reasons why I am in Saudi Arabia with my young family and not in my Brooklyn. Some may object to capital punishment, but I object to living with subhuman maniacs. Furthermore, the public spectacle I witnessed earlier undoubtedly deters the crazies and offers a clear example to the sane folk, like myself.

The execution is called "Hudoodullah" or "The Punishment of Allah" and that is deep to think about. Just imagine having the punishment of whom you believe to be the Creator inflicted on you. Man's punishment, imprisonment, doesn't seem to stop people from committing horrendous crimes, but maybe if they started taking the heads of murderous gangbangers, serial killers, rapists and others who are proven guilty without a shadow of a doubt and admit guilt, then the children of NYC and the entire USA would be able to play outside past midnight unsupervised. Just a thought.

For the record, the family of the victim has the right to spare the life of the criminal and demand blood money or payment for the offense. In addition, the criminals are due a trial with the evidences presented by the prosecution during which time the criminal is imprisoned. There is a long list of legal procedures done prior to the execution of a criminal. The man who I witnessed earlier was not dragged from the van and he did not seem to outwardly object his fate. He kneeled down on command and took his beheading.

I am still processing what I witnessed and one more time for good measure, WOW. But I do feel safer here than I have ever felt in the States. Go figure.

With New Eyes

An excerpt from my journal, my immediate reactions to witnessing a beheading still amaze me over 5 years later. If there was any single moment standing out the most from my years abroad it was the beheading. Many things left me in awe, but none gripped me as much as seeing a man's head leave his body. Despite the time that has passed the mere thought of that day still makes the hairs on my neck raise.

Since then beheadings have made their way into the news due to extremists in the Middle East. These misguided extremists have allegedly beheaded hostages from foreign lands as well as citizens in the lands they have commandeered. It must be noted that what I observed was vastly different from the extremist beheadings. First and most important, what I witnessed is unanimously agreed upon as being in the appropriate punishment for said crime in an Islamic country governed by the legislative texts. On the other hand, the kidnapping and execution of nonMuslims and Muslims for ransom has no textual basis in Islam.

Also, the extremists, again in direct opposition of textual Islamic mandates, execute inhumanely. In some instance, they have beheading with a Rambo styled combat knife, which is nowhere near the clean kill offered by the bowed Saudi sword. Granted, my Islamic faith makes me biased with delineating between the two, but without a doubt, there are differences. The last difference between the two is: the rapist was guilty of crime while those who have been beheading by the extremists were not in fact guilty of any offense. Yet in still, the prospect of witnessing this type of execution may put off many Americans, despite the fact the media is apt to commonly broadcast footage of killings, some that have come by the hands of the police.

Between news outlets and the internet, many have watched tragic accidents and brutal crimes that have lead up to death; however, the idea of watching an execution is somewhat out of reach to the average American and therein laid my curiosity to see such a spectacle. Since travelling was all about seeing the never before seen, watching a criminal lose his head was as new to me as seeing herds of camels walking along the highways, but a bit more extreme.

Years later, I still refuse to go into the political issues attached to capital punishment because I still understand its usefulness. That argument set aside, I can still feel myself standing at the parking lot on that hot September day paralyzed by the shock of what I had just witnessed. To my amazement, I was able to, albeit, briefly digest the event just enough then write about it in my journal later that night, but aside from that no further clarity has come to me since that ominous day. Being no stranger to death and crime, I find it strange that I still cannot process that execution. Years have passed, but the time has yet to offer me any wisdom. To an extent, just as the body of the executed remained in the lotus position after his head was cut off is exactly how I am frozen in perspective about that day.

As a Muslim, our approach to death is a bit different from the average Western take. Muslims live day to day with a constant reminder that each day can be one's last. In many of our invocations, we ask for a refuge from death and some of the matters directly pertaining to it. We understand that death is inevitable and every soul will taste it. As opposed to ignoring the inevitable until it can no longer ignored, we keep the reminder fresh with the intent of praying every prayer like it is our last and taking advantage of time, good health, and the other blessings bestowed on us with life. Rather than the macabre callousness that is expected, our paradigm offers perspective geared towards encouraging us to live out each day in the best possible manner because we accept that death is near to us all.

As this psychology relates to the execution, I feel my understanding of the immediacy and finality of death was cemented. Within a blink, the convicted criminal's life was no longer and the world kept turning. This is the case with death. Perhaps the learn-able moment, for me, can be found in knowing that all actions are followed by reactions and some actions will inevitably leads to one's own demise.

The People of the Gulf

Aside from the questions about the safety of living in the Gulf, my friends in the States would always ask about the Arab, particularly how they treated me. Being well aware of the realization that most New Yorkers only are exposed to the Arabs who own the majority of delis in New York City, this line of questioning came as no surprise. Outside of that corner store contact, most information about Middle Easterners and their culture comes by way of media reports on events in the Middle East and the ever-continuous coverage on those nut jobs called Extremists.

On the other hand, my experience with the people of that region was a bit more in-depth than the average American because of my faith and the multi-ethnic mosque I grew up in. As a result, I was already very familiar with the people and their customs, to some degree. The great pride they took in treating the guest with care and respect, as well as, their eagerness to share food and give gifts to travelers and their neighbors were made known to me while in America but, of course, not to the degree of what I came across while in the Middle East.

For example, during my first extended stay in Saudi Arabia, my neighbor surprised me with a delightfully exquisite dinner I can still taste years later. On an uneventful day a few days after my arrival my doorbell rang then after answering the door I was greeted by my neighbor who then handed me a large platter of freshly steamed and fried fish with rice and fresh vegetables. The neighbor then immediately bid me farewell, only to walk away as I stood in the doorway holding the platter looking confused without having the chance to thank him. Never had I experienced anything like that in New York City or in the South, where hospitality grows on trees and floats through the air like pollen in the spring. Thoroughly impressed and very much appreciative of the surprise dinner, that was my introduction to the People of the Gulf in their own land.

To me, understanding a people without understanding their tongue is similar to watching a movie with no audio. While it is true that gestures and body language are forms of communication, but they lack the ability to convey the detail of a spoken or signed language. If I wanted to truly get a feel for the people, I would have to be able to communicate with them. Luckily for me, growing up in as an American in a Muslim community in afforded me the opportunity to attend a small private Islamic school where as a child I learned the Arabic alphabet, how to read and correctly pronounce the letters with the exact detail Arabic demands. Aside from using formal Arabic greetings as well as memorizing a few chapters from the Quran, I did not know how to communicate in Arabic despite being able to read, write and correctly pronounce the language. Due to this, immediately after my arrival in the Gulf I began to dive head first into studying how to converse in the Arabic language. It was already made known to me through my childhood classes that Arabic was a tongue of many intricacies. Each letter and vowel is always given its rights without any slacking or omission. In Arabic, there is no "tomayto, tomahto" nor is there the slurring of letters into an informal slang. Actually, there is something like that but those alterations exclusively belong to the numerous Arabic dialects in their respective countries.

In my efforts to gain as strong of a command of the language as possible I sought the services of some of the locals but I had a hard time finding a native speaker who spoke the formal language with rules of grammar because most natives speak in a local dialect. Eventually, I was advised to take classes on an internet based language center teacher located in Egypt. The language center gave my classes twice a week, by way of Skype, while I was in Saudi Arabia. Why would I pay an Egyptian in Egypt to teach me Arabic while I was in Saudi Arabia? Well, I was advised to do so because the Egyptians are known for being good teachers of Arabic grammar; a positive stereotype, if ever there is a thing. Legend and history states that Al-Azhar University in Cairo Egypt was once the global center for studying Arabic and Islamic Sciences. Students from all over the world would go to Egypt to learn Arabic, which in turn led to many of the locals freelancing as Arabic tutors. This traditional side hustle has carried on for generations branding the Egyptians as the go-to teachers for Arabic in the Middle East. Egypt was also the pioneer of media, in both film and music, which spread through the Arabian Gulf making the Egyptian dialect of Arabic the most commonly understood among Arabs from other countries. Since the Egyptian dialect is well-known, it is common to see Egyptian teachers instructing in their own dialect to students fluent in another dialect. As a result, the Egyptians have the reputation of being great teachers, so I went along with the flow.

I was learning the standard Arabic and for that I needed a teacher who knew the rules of grammar in addition to the other sciences of Arabic, so after I found my guy then spent some time in class, I grew comfortable speaking with my teacher. Every class started with a small conversation about my daily affairs. Once while practicing Arabic conversation with my native speaking teacher, who was also versed in grammar, I was questioned about my students in Saudi? I responded, "They are all....", then my teacher stopped me immediately saying; "Don't make generalizations." I agreed then thought to myself, I was being advised not to make generalizations by a teacher I chose because of a generalization. This was very ironic, but his advice was sound; this I cannot object, even though sometimes it is easier said than done.

Fast forward to my return home to the States, just as during my time abroad, my American friends always asked me about the people of the Gulf. Questions like, "How are they?", "Are they nice?", or "Are they racist?" were the most common and the most difficult to answer, if only because people are complex. Generally, the locals were very nice and welcoming to me. I did meet assholes occasionally, however I blame those individuals not their fellow citizens as an entire people. I did observe and experience some social customs I thought to be less than Islamic or even bearing any semblance of what I thought was good manners, but that judgment is biased because it was foreign to the culture in question. If you're following, it is clear to see how difficult these questions are to answer. The best I can offer is my opinion based on my experiences and observations.

The people were merely people. They were obviously different from Westerners, by way of culture, but they seemed to be just like us. Those with money obviously enjoyed the finer things such as palatial villas, high-end luxury cars, and designer fashions. There was no discernible difference between the wealthy in America and the wealthy of the Gulf Region. Rich is rich everywhere and that is absolute. The poorer folk were quite different though. Their faces and attitude were void of despair and angst. To me, they seemed to be dignified yet humble and gracious with their condition all without being entirely content. This was an oddity to me coming from a low-income area where I was used to seeing the less fortunate looking sad, stressed, and depressed. This was not the case in the Gulf, where despite the immense wealth; there are also extremely poor people, of Arab descent as well as nonArabs. The poor Middle Easterners had no proverbial dark cloud hovering over their heads, which were not hung over in sadness. They were happy. Obviously not happy about being poor, they were happy about whatever they could be happy about and it resonated loudly.

The middle class lifestyle, however, was a bit ritzier than America due to cheaper domestic labor. A person with a government position or any field that requires a four-year degree can usually afford to have a live-in maid or a driver. This is the norm.

One constant that I encountered with virtually everyone in the Gulf, regardless of class, was their deep understanding of love and bond with their family. For them, kinship was cherished, appreciated, and honored. This was made obvious to me very early after I found out about a custom where the entire family meets for dinner the night before the workweek begins. What we have in America as yearly family reunions, they have as weekly Sunday dinners. I thought that to be very endearing and, quite possibly, more in line with how things used to be done in the past when times were much simpler. On the opposite end of the spectrum, those strong family bonds also led to many students being absent because of a sicknesses or deaths in the families. At first, I thought they were running game on me because lateness and/or absence due to family sickness was a weekly occurrence for most students, then I learned about their custom of sitting with sick family members and that their families are usually much, much larger. A larger family meant more sick people or perhaps a student being responsible for shuttling family members to and from the hospital to see the sick relative. Honestly, I was floored and jealous my society wasn't nearly as family centered. There were even times when I called out of work to care for my wife, at the time, who was not feeling well. In America, I would have had to call in faking a sickness as we have different norms of what are acceptable reasons for calling out of work. The people and society of the Gulf, overall, seemed to have more of a concern for the family structure. I respect it to the utmost.

In regards to my students in Saudi Arabia, they were usually college-aged during the day with the working professionals, seeking to brush up on their English for career purposes, attending at night. The college-aged students were almost like high schoolers in America; not because of immaturity, but because they had an undeniable innocence in their demeanor as well as in their eyes. Perhaps not being exposed to as much sheltered them from all the things that makes the youth grow up so quickly in the States. They have had a childhood without dealing with many of the social issues prevalent in America. Drugs, gang violence, along with the sorrow and callousness they both cause are not issues in the Arabian Gulf Coast countries as they are in the States. They have also been sheltered from over-sexualized media. Again, I was jealous. Not only are the youth allowed to be carefree longer, it is customary for the children to live at the parent's home up until marriage then move out. They do not leave home to move into their own places to have freedom as we do in America.

The reality is the average early 20s-ish Gulf citizen has zero responsibilities except for maybe a car payment. When all things were considered, it was easy to see why my college-aged students were still so wet behind the ears. They were still kids, by American standards. As I engaged and observed my students even more, I noticed many of them would use roses and poetry memes as avatars on instant messengers and social media. While the average American young adult male in the same age range would never expose himself as a hopeless romantic for fear of teasing from other guys, this sort of behavior was common amongst the young Gulf guys. They were legitimately looking for love. With American my eyes, this was another odd sight to see. Looking at it from their angle, their culture calls for marriage instead of boyfriend/girlfriend relationships, so they sought out what was socially acceptable. Those young men were interested in something a bit more substantial than a fun time. Yet another positive characteristic noted and respected.

While in Kuwait, the majority of my students were working professionals, many of whom had advanced degrees in the various sciences. Among my students were lawyers, doctors, engineers, even a professor. My position as an instructor of an "Advanced Conversational English" allowed for the format of my classes to consist mainly of conversations of substance. Initially, foreign language learners learn how to communicate in everyday situations, but advanced students aim to express themselves about a variety of worldly topics in the target language. A traveler moonlighting as a teacher, I used this opportunity to guide my students through conversations comparing Arab customs and ideals versus what they knew about Western culture. It was through their conversations, which I moderated, I was able to get a real feel for the working person in the Gulf.

Since my course was "Advanced Conversational English", they expressed a wide array of hopes and fears for themselves and their children. To my surprise, those worries were as regular as the average Americans minus the regular violence and drugs that we in America are constantly exposed to in either real life or through media reports. One student, Mirat, was a married Christian Egyptian physician with two high school aged children. She seemed to have the normal concerns of a working wife with teenagers. She worried about her children not getting good grades and falling in with the wrong crowd. Ebrahim was a Kuwaiti married, middle-aged petroleum engineer with children. Like Mirat and most working parents, his concerns were centered on his career, his children's education, and getting enough rest. It seemed to me that despite differing cultures there are always common traits that will be present in most people. The realization that: "People are, in fact, people" was cemented with each meaningful conversation I was blessed to engage in with the locals.

Conversely, one major difference between American culture and Gulf culture was that discussing or referring to an ethnicity and/or race was not a taboo. It is a regular practice, on that side of the world, to inquire about a person's nationality and ethnicity or country of origin. Nothing is inferred from it. If I went into a conversation with a local while speaking Arabic I was immediately asked about my nationality. After I replied that I am an American, I was then questioned about my country of origin because my tongue as an American Arabic speaker sounded as if perhaps my parents could have been Arab. Almost all of the locals I met hit me with that line of questions soon after the introductory greeting. Soon I grew to expect it and took no offense because the traveler is more often than not, nothing but a stranger. Asking a question about a stranger is very normal no matter where a person is from.

In Middle Eastern culture, conversations about race and ethnicity were acceptable in casual conversation but also in a professional setting. For instance, the average resume for a job seeker on that side of the world includes the job hunter's nationality; this is customary. While job-hunting in Kuwait, I secured a position an English Language Center for the aforementioned position. After being hired, I received a call from Human Resources questioning me about my ethnicity because despite being an American my name is Arabic and the students specifically paid for a native English speaker. The caller was an Egyptian with a Canadian passport, but he needed to make sure I was, in fact, actually an American and not a naturalized citizen like he was. The mere reality of preferential treatment in the job market supports the presence of discrimination and prejudice, by American definition, but in that culture, it seemed to be something different.

In a place like Kuwait, which is a very small country with a very large foreign population of 60%, mechanisms or barriers are set in place to make sure the native minority remains in a favorable position. Perks such as free housing, education, and food discounts were only for the Kuwaitis. Furthermore, the natives can only hold certain jobs and likewise there are other jobs that are normally reserved for foreigners. This is their system.

While it isn't an equal opportunity system, it does work for its citizens.

In reality, I learned that the people of The Gulf are a bit more transparent with their biases, which is double-edged sword. On one hand, I can appreciate being told up front if there is an issue without having to "sense a vibe" then allege that a person or institution is being discriminatory of my race or faith without having concrete proof. On the other hand, it is a very bitter pill to swallow when being told you cannot live in a certain area because it is reserved for a certain nationality, which I encountered while apartment hunting in Kuwait. In fact, real estate listings on that side of the world will advertise the preferred nationality of prospective tenants in the ads. Again, in their culture this is accepted, but is not the only way business is handled. All of my flats in Saudi were in neighborhoods where I was one of few foreigners residing there, while in Kuwait I simply couldn't afford to live in Kuwaiti suburbs due to my position not offering a housing allowance, however I had American friends who did. Conversely, in attempting to see it through their eyes, it made sense to me that certain property owners who were looking for upscale tenants would request American applicants because, more than likely, the positions held by Westerners would cover the rent without any issues. We seem to have a good reputation for paying rent in full while living in these countries. It is also assumed that Westerners work for a company that, by law, is required to provide a housing stipend and this holds usually holds true. Perhaps, as a way to entice foreign workers, both laborers and specialized professions to work there, the oil rich countries mandate that employers pay for their employees to live there; some companies had housing while others would give a housing allowance to cover living expenses. After weighing everything from their perspective, I could see why certain nationalities were sought in residential ads. Of course, in America, this would be considered a discriminatory practice, however this was not America.

In addition, I later learned of the concern from some locals in having foreign strangers in their neighborhood where their children and wives were. One such instance occurred in my 2nd year abroad while in Abha, Saudi Arabia. While outside of a local mosque and after attending one of the daily congregational prayers I was approached by an older Saudi man in his 60s inquiring about my identity (nationality) and occupation. In a nutshell, the man told me to my face, that he was curious because I was a stranger in their community. He wanted to know who I was and who my employer was then he said to me, "This is because my family is here." His family referred to his wife or wives and female offspring or relatives. In traditional Arab culture, there are certain etiquettes afforded to the neighbor as well as inter-gender taboos. Simply put, a man has no good reason speaking to the wife or daughters of another man. Barring foreigners from certain sub-communities ensured the locals some semblance of cultural continuity. I am not mad at them for this. I understand that it is not fair and it goes against certain American principles, but I was not in America. Furthermore, I am not the guest who dares to tell his host how he should decorate his own home.

The reality of the matter, based solely on my perception and experiences, cannot be ignored, however, judgment is withheld. Moreover, in all honesty, living on that side of world was pretty damn comfortable despite certain barriers. For the most part, the locals have found a way to preserve their traditional way of living whilst making the meat of the foreign labor force at ease.

In understanding that no man made social system is infallible, there are some kinks that need to be worked out, not just in the Middle East, but everywhere inhabited by humankind. People are ultimately people that tend to feel most comfortable around others with similar upbringings, backgrounds, and ideals. However, I feel the best of people treat their guests with respect and open arms while the best guest do their utmost to respect and not disturb the routines of the host, whether that host is a person or a place. Wherever in the world I travel my intent is to see the good in the locals while trying to understand their way of thinking. By putting myself in their shoes I see them as I see myself. This is how I make the best out of my experiences away from home. Definitively, how do I feel about the people of the countries I stayed in and frequented? I lived the locals for almost 4 years straight without returning to America and would love to do it again when the opportunity presents itself. That's how I feel.

THE N WORD YET AGAIN

Up until this point, I had been in the Kingdom for over a year and a half. I was functional with the language allowing me to spend more time with the locals interacting in order to get a better feel for the place. The culture shock never completely died down, but it did reach a steady level of shock and surprise which meant I was pretty much adjusted. In the spirit of being social, a very wealthy student invited the staff to his estate for a barbeque where I came across the N word yet again.

While becoming acquainted with everyone in attendance, I met a Black man in his 30s who turned out to be from Yemen. Yemen is a small, poor Arab country to the south of Saudi Arabia and is responsible for breeding the entrepreneurial men who have taken over every corner store deli in New York City. In fact, every Yemeni I met while in the Middle East had a cousin working in and/or owning a store in America. It seems that industry has aided their people very, very well. Anyhow, after talking to the

Black guy, who happened to be half-Yemeni and half-Somali, for a brief moment he offered an observation about me in Arabic.

He said to me, "Anta Sha'neen." *Translates to "You are sha'neen."*

I responded, "Maa   m'ana   sha'neen. *Translates to "What does sha'neen mean?*

He says, "You know like street......gang......like nigga."

My colleague who attended the barbeque with me and I immediately busted out laughing because it was hilarious. In asking him why did he think that about me, he replied that it was because of how I walk and talk. It was funny to me because the Yemeni was just a black as me in skin tone and he also had an undeniably urban demeanor, but I am actually from the rough hoods of NYC while he was from a village in Yemen. The pot had just called the kettle black.

He then told me how his mother is Black (Somali) so he's Black. Oddly, most dark olive toned Arabs with kinky hair will claim Arab even if they would be considered Black by American standards, but this guy was indeed very different from his fellow Arabs. Since most dark skinned Arabs, normally, do not like being called Black, I came across an oddity in finding one proudly claiming Black as if heard James Brown's classic record, "I'm Black & I'm Proud". He later admitted to me that he was "Shway Majnoon" or "A little bit crazy" and of course everyone within earshot concurred. The Black Yemeni was quite the black sheep, but he was exactly he is the kind of cool people I prefer to keep company with.

About the "N" Word

Discussions about the N word and its usage are not new. Within the Black and Hip-Hop communities, we have been tossing around the word quite frequently for some time despite its ugly inception. The "N" word did have a disparaging meaning initially, but the prevalent meaning and most popular usage has gradually changed over time. In fact, this change in meaning, a semantic shift, is not a phenomenon new to language. Old words with new meanings are plentiful in English because the language permits the popular meaning winning out thus hijacking the word. For instance, nice meant silly at one time just as awful meant full or worthy of awe. Fathom once meant to encircle with one's arms. A myriad referred specifically to a bunch of things numbering at 10,000 while hussies originally meant a housewife. As we can see, linguistically it is acceptable, but socially there are some issues that need to be addressed. And, yes, that was an understatement.

We, of the Hip-Hop generation, are fully aware of the history of the "N" word, just as we know the usage of the word offends some, but our Hip-Hop generation and culture, in large, really doesn't care. I cannot count how many classic Hip-Hop songs there are with the N word and I won't count, because we don't care, for the most part. It's obvious because the word is everywhere. Admittedly so, many do not use the word, however the majority rules. If those who are against using it were of the majority than the overall usage of the N word would phase out. And yes, that was also an oversimplification, but it would be hard to argue against it.

Ultimately, a word only has a much power as you give it, yet the history of the word "nigger" is an account too horrid and profound to ever forget. However, the word "nigga" has traveled to parts of the world the where a once self-professed "Hood Nigga" has never traveled. The definition has also made leaps, never thought of before even by those who most commonly and affectionately use the word. To be the descendant of a slave who was undoubtedly called "Nigger" while being from the Hip-Hop generation that uses the word "nigga" like surfers use the word "dude"" to then, in turn, be informed of a new definition, of something so intimate, by someone so foreign was just outrageous. Surreal fits the feeling best.

Quite honestly, almost every young Middle Eastern person I encountered, who was a hip-hop fan, asked me about the "N" word to such an extent it almost became an expected conversation. Most were generally confused about it because they vaguely knew of the word's origins, but still heard it all the time in music. Others were die-hard hip-hop fans who perhaps might have not known about the culture in-depth, but really dug their teeth into whatever they came across.

One such young man was named Zayd, spoke with his best urban American accent in an attempt to pass off as being other than an Arab, but I wasn't fooled. I kept asking him about his nationality because his tongue was definitely Arab. By the time I met Zayd, I had been teaching English to various leveled students for 3 years, as a result my ears were able to pick on the small pronunciation mistakes the native Arabic speaker usually made when speaking English. Zayd was damn good as an English speaker, but my ears were clearly better. After trying to pass off as an American he eventually admitted to being a Kuwaiti, much to my surprise. Despite his Kuwaiti nationality and Arab ethnicity, Zayd was adamant about referring to himself as Black.

Reminiscent of the ethno-conscious fervor of some of my people in the States, Zayd was Black; the end. To prove his point, he pulled out his cell phone with pictures of his Black Kuwaiti family, all of different hues, most of which were visually Black by Western standards. Zayd continued on about his Blackness seemingly for an eternity then admitted to being a "Nigga" because he loves Hip-Hop, but not because he is Black. Surreal.

Prior to this experience, I would have never known that in some parts of the Middle East, a nigga is nothing more than a fly Hip-Hop dude, and a compliment for most who know of the word. Go figure.

Oddities

My hometown, New York City, is known to be a melting pot. Without a doubt, I credit my acceptance of all things diverse to growing up in a city with so many different ethnic sub-communities and minorities. As a child, one of my family's favorite dine-in restaurants was quaint restaurant in Boerum Hill named "The India House". Once inside the scents and sounds of India enveloped the patrons transporting them to a foreign continent, leaving behind all things New York upon entry. In lower Manhattan there is a Chinatown, where the Chinese immigrants have settled. Many shops in this area have awnings in Cantonese while the Russian community has their own neighborhood in the Brighton Beach, Brighton Beach.

It was in this melting pot I grew from a curious boy to a highly inquisitive man. In fact, I had become so used to diversity that attempts to live in other cities throughout the States never really panned out because they lacked the variety which shaped me. One can only tolerate so much Olive Garden, Golden Corral and Waffle House before craving a Trinidadian roti or double with tamarind sauce. To its detriment, being from a melting pot gave me a false sense of security as if I've experienced everything under the sun. Eventually, I would come to learn differently.

The new understanding I was presented with informed me that merely being exposed to some aspects of different foreign cultures does not compare to being totally submersed, which is, in fact, to be consumed and surrounded by a new culture. At every angle and turn there was something interesting, odd, amazing and new to learn and understand. Without a doubt, there were many facets about the cultures of the Middle East that were somewhat odd to Hip-Hop kid from New York City. One such instance occurred immediately after exiting the plane in Jeddah, Saudi Arabia where I had observed couples of men holding hands while walking about in the terminal. Reminiscent of two lovers in the park on a nice spring day, it was an emphatically unforeseen sight. It was not just one or two couples of men doing this; it seemed to be the entire terminal. Confused is not the word, for I thought I had just entered a Pride parade in Greenwich Village. Well, maybe it was not that extreme, but it was still a very, very odd sight when one considers Saudi Arabia is known to be ultra-conservative. Were the press reports of the strict Islamic state exaggerated or was there something explaining the phenomenon of young men casually holding hands? Once I made contact with a few fellow Americans, the first thing I asked about was the men holding hands.

"Yo, what's up with these dudes holding each others hand?"

At that moment, I was informed that it was a cultural gesture. Apparently, it is normal for close male friends and relatives to hold hands while strolling about. This was not just an Arab thing as I had observed Bengali, Indians, Sudanese, and other Africans doing the very same thing.

"Wow. That's different. Well, better believe I won't be holding any man's hand. Get outta here wit that"

My response was that of the average American male. No matter how cool or close we are, we just do not hold hands. We don't do that, at all.

Months went by before the shock of seeing men holding hands dissipated, but ever so often, while with an American friend, we would see it then chuckle. It's a part of their culture, so we just withheld judgment then continued on in The Twilight Zone known as submersion in a foreign culture.

Perhaps a year after arriving in Saudi Arabia, I was began to do business with a local young man who acted as a liaison, carrying out municipal duties for me such as visa renewal. He was a friend of my family who had already been settled in the Kingdom for more than a decade, so he immediately had a familiarity with me even though he really did not know me personally. In many other cultures outside of America people are known by their families. This means that knowing a person's family is a criteria for knowing a person. I guess the old adage of an apple not falling far from the trees rings true around the world. Since I needed my visas renewed, I invited the young twenty something year old Saudi to my home to detail exactly what was needed. When he entered, I observed the local customs when dealing with a guest. I brought him a platter with water, tea, and some sweets then we discussed business. We went over the details then I escorted him out to his car, but while in the elevator the young calmly reached out then held my hand. A first time moment for me, my mind began to immediately race.

"Oh S**t, he is holding my hand. Yo, what the f**k?"

My nerves were all over the place. I felt weird; this was a very unusual moment for me. Despite my own cultural leanings, I did not pull away because I understood the gesture, so I left my hand inside his then acted as if everything normal setting aside the thoughts racing through my head.

"Okay. Calm down. You're holding hands with a man. It doesn't mean you're sleeping with him. It's just holding hands. It's innocent. There's nothing to worry about"

The experience was quite strange. His hands were surprisingly smooth and gentle. Why this was a surprise escapes me but I was definitely shocked. As we exited my apartment building hand in hand I could not wait to let go of his hand. Yes, I am diverse and I love experiencing new cultures, but this was a tad bit too much for child of the overly macho Hip-Hop culture. Once we reached his car, we released hands then did the customary farewell. When I returned to my flat I told my ex-wife that the Saudi guy held my hand and, of course, she belted out laughing. She sensed I was a bit uncomfortable by the experience but that didn't stop her from letting out the signature Wendy Williams catchphrase "How you dooooin'" which in response led me to laugh as well. While there were many aspects of other cultures I consciously chose to adapt into my own life, holding another man's hand won't be one of them. I respect it, but I will leave that with the people who were reared with that practice. I'm good.

When I boarded my flight leaving America I had no idea that one of my most unforgettable moments abroad would come by way of walking hand in hand with another man. Similarly, while holding the young Saudis hand, it did not register that the oddities come in levels. During my last year abroad as an expatriate living in Kuwait, I befriended a few guys from the local East African community. Kuwait has a sizable Ethiopian and Somali population. While I had made friends with a bunch of Somalis with British nationality living in Saudi Arabia, I never had the chance to sit amongst the Ethiopians even though my paternal grandfather was an Ethiopian. One day while exploring my neighborhood, I happened upon a shop with a big Bob Marley poster in the window. "Weird", I thought to myself. If I were in the Flabush section of Brooklyn, I would have paid the poster no mind, but in that area of the world the poster stood out like a sore thumb. I entered the shop then was greeted by stunning Ethiopian young woman in her mid twenties. After glancing around the shop seemed to sell spices and other items imported from Ethiopia for their local contingent in Kuwait. Almost immediately I questioned the young woman regarding where all Ethiopians hang out to which she directed me to a hookah lounge a few doors down.

In the following weeks, this Ethiopian hookah lounge became my after work hangout spot. Eventually and as expected, I made friendly with the other patrons most of whom were East African or Sudanese. We would share stories about our homelands while buying each other tea or hookah, for those who smoked, and we also shared finger foods like popcorn. Inside the lounge was also a PS4 soccer video game that many of us would play to past time.

One night at the lounge started as routine as any other; the Arab men were flirting with the Ethiopian ladies, the Ethiopian men joked loudly amongst one another, the

Sudanese men smoked cigarettes and drank tea, etc. The lounge was bustling. At the corner where I sat I was were three Ethiopian women, a Kuwaiti dude who happened to be a Rastafarian, and an Ethiopian man. We were all being social, as we normally did, when the idea to order something to eat was brought up. In consensus, we all agreed then a call was made to a nearby Ethiopian restaurant for the meal. After 10 minutes, the dish we ordered was delivered, so it was time to dig in.

Up until that point, I had eaten a couple of Ethiopian dishes. The injeera bread, which is a staple in their diet, reminded me of crepes but without the fruity toppings. While some of the spices were reminiscent of those dishes I had sampled from West African cultures, namely a Nigerian grilled beef dish called Seeray. The dish we ate was called Tibs. It was lightly fried morsels of meat and vegetable eaten with the traditional injeera bread along with an assortment of spices to dip the meat with bread into. As soon as the giant platter was delivered, everyone began picking at it with their hands; after all is was finger food similar to buffalo wings at an American bar.

Since this was my first time eating with Ethiopians I was patient to observe their table manners and customs before joining the meal in order to not do something awkwardly American. My patience and observation allowed me to catch wind of something, which I wasn't sure if it a custom or just good friends being close with each other while eating. What I observed were the people at the table picking up the small morsels of meat then placing it in the mouths of others. Was it something that this group of friend did as an inside joke or was it a a custom of their people? First, I saw the women do it to each other followed by the Ethiopian dude doing it to one of the women. I had thought to myself that this was a very charming custom if that, in fact, is what it was. My admiration was quickly interrupted with realization that someone would soon be placing a chunk of the fried aromatic meat in my mouth. Of course, I was game because those moments experiencing other than the customary New York occurrences, if there is a such thing, make travelling so appealing to me. After everything had registered I turned my attention away from the table for a brief moment then when I turned my head back around the Ethiopian man was picking up a piece of meat. Thinking nothing of it, he raised his hand towards my face then placed the meat in my mouth. A custom reserved for lovers and parents in my country was common table etiquette another, however, understanding this still didn't remove the awkwardness I felt in knowing a man just hand fed me. It was a super odd moment that will be remembered for the rest of my life.

My time abroad was packed full of moments like this one and with unique individuals, such as the Kuwaiti Rastafarian seated at the table in the aforementioned meal. A rotund, Arab man is late 20s; Yaqub was the most unique Arab I had met while in the Middle East because before him I had never met an Arab Rasta. For all intensive purposes, I believe he was more of a Rasta in appearance than in belief, yet this was still quite amazing. His locked hair flowed down his back, but like most Rastas he usually wore it in a large knitted hat. As he and I grew closer, he explained to me that he frequently traveled to Ethiopia, where he had a wife and he was fluent in the Ethiopian tongue Amharic. To say I was amazed is an understatement. He also shared with me some of the struggles he faced with the traditional Kuwaitis because of his appearance, which was more Rasta culture than Kuwaiti culture. The brother Yaqub was quite the oddity in a very good way and he helped make my time in Kuwait quite smooth and livable.

What I call oddities were nothing more than those unfathomable new experiences and personalities I encountered. Through those experiences and personalities, I was forced into accepting a new reality of greater depths, much richer than anything I had ever thought of. Those oddities grew me and I'm grateful.

The Return

On June 30 2013, with 3 large suitcases and a multi-colored backpack, I boarded a plane at Kuwait International Airport. My destination was a place I had not been in 40 months, or 3and a half years. I was finally returning home to New York City after the most amazing journey I had ever experienced in my still young life. My flight, the cheapest one possible, had a layover in Riyadh, Saudi Arabia. How befitting that I would be forced to spend another 9 hours in Saudi Arabia in order to return to the US. My Saudi experience was one that was bittersweet. Amazing moments were dampened by a handful of rotten apples, however, I graciously took the bad with the good, so no love was lost nor were any ill feelings harbored because Saudi grew me immensely, yet in still I was forced to spend a long layover in a less than comfortable airport.

My connecting flight to New York's JFK airport lasted almost 15 hours. I cannot recall much from the flight perhaps due to my anxiousness in returning to the home I had long had a love/hate relationship. My love was none other than the love a man feels for the place that birthed and raised him. My hate stood rooted in knowing my city and perhaps my country was not able to offer the enrichment I so desperately had desired for my growth and more so, my ability to live life with life. Despite this there I was on a cross Atlantic flight foolishly and so arrogantly attempting to make sense of the last 3 and half years of my life. Considering it took me well over six months to begin to articulate my first 6 week stay in the Middle East in 2008; for me to sum up the whole of my experience during a flight was as futile an effort as one could muster. I needed time to gain that perspective I sought. I needed time to readjust to my own city and the people's unique brand of Gotham hospitality. A year later, in front of my laptop I carefully type my offering as I finally feel the clarity I sought has been achieved. As difficult as it was to adjust then submerge myself into a foreign culture was the trial of my reentry and readjustment to all things New York and on a larger scale American.

In my first weeks home I was a tourist of sorts finding myself marveling at the Times Square lights I had frequented on many of weekends as a teenager. The photos I shared on my social networks were also in the vein of a tourist. Fire trucks, the subway, yellow cabs, the former World Trade Center, all of which were at one time so mundane to me, were now spectacles to be captured for eternity. I was, in effect, a foreigner even though I was as American as apple pie. Being new was not necessarily new to me, but being new here, in my own city, was definitely something had never experienced. As Nelson Mandela said, "After one climbs a mountain, he finds yet another mountain to climb." I had reached the summit only encounter yet another mountain in the unlikely places; my home city.

Things changed greatly in NYC since I left some time ago. My old hood, Bed-Stuy, was no longer a hood due to gentrification. Inflation had risen the prices of common items I would normal buy. A hero sandwich that I used to purchase for $3.50, were now closer to six dollars. In addition, the trusty hustles, which kept me afloat prior to my jaunt, were dried up, not mention my list of local contacts was almost nonexistent as many had moved away while a handful passed away. There I was starting from scratch in the city were at one time I was able to enjoy midtown spa treatments on a whim followed by solitary brunches at one of the many sidewalk cafes. I was out of sync as well as out of the loop. I took a sometime job as mover, which I found through a hook-up with a childhood friend with whom I had reconnected. The work was easy yet not enough to maintain my fill; also the job didn't offer any semblance of stimulation my newly acquired sensibilities yearned for. My co-workers were not like the people I worked with in Saudi Arabia and Kuwait. In the Middle East, I shared a unique bond with my fellow teachers, if only because they were on the same journey I had embarked on as an American living and working abroad.

Whether I had a deeper connection with those men and women from the US, Canada, Britain, South Africa, and all places native to the English language, wasn't important. What was important was that we all had shared an ambitious fearlessness, which allowed us to implant ourselves then submerse in a polarizing culture, far different from our own. While abroad, I was certain to be in the company of fellow aliens, those of whom were willing to not only think, but also leap outside of the box. On the other hand, my coworkers at my new job were far more R2D2 than ET, thus robbing me of the necessity to be around those who push and inspire me. Good people they were, they just were not fully my people. The sense I had wished to make of my time abroad began to envelop me at that time. After months of inconsistent work as mover, I had changed employment to work as a truck in and around Long Island, Queens, the Bronx, and Manhattan. Though I was not travelling to new cultures, the ability to circumnavigate my city appealed to me greatly. The money was very good but the hours were extremely long, sometimes 60+ hours in a five-day workweek. The work involved collecting donations from homes for various charitable organizations then transporting those donations to sorting facilities throughout the city. The work was as unexciting as it sounds; nonetheless, the pay was great even if I was deprived of sleep, a social life, and time to invest to future endeavors. Essentially the job was a well paying dead end gig. Extremely grateful for the provisions bestowed upon me, I approached each day with gratitude even though the job did nothing for me on a deeper level. I had learned long ago that money, no matter how large the sum, could never take the place of pure happiness.

Often my Saturdays were spent revisiting the Union Square Soho areas where I made a name for myself selling cds during the time I aspired to be a rapper. On some of the same corners that paid my rent, I stood reflecting while watching the shoppers make their rounds, the vendors peddle their wares and the latest wave of aspiring rappers sell their music. As expected, watching the hustling emcees brought back warm memories from when I defied the odds to my own beat. That same spirit pushed me to make the leap overseas doing what some considered crazy. In all honesty, I missed selling my cds and the virtual freedom I felt. So, with the job I soldiered on day after day, week after week until road fatigue caused me to have an accident that led to me losing my job.

Fast forward, almost a year later, my transition back to being a New Yorker has been terrible. Unfortunately, the city that never sleeps consumed me sending me spiraling in a funk, which later turned into a depression. To go from a safe society where I was in no threat of being robbed or killed by police to a place where one must constantly be vigilant was more a bit much to bear. I found myself not being motivated to do things that I love to do in addition to being grumpy overall. If that wasn't a new mountain to climb then I did not know what was.

This project seemed to help me pull myself back together by, I guess, culminating the whole of my experience into something that makes sense. Perhaps that is a reach but the fact is I still have not fully made sense of those wonderful yet trying 4 years of my life. All I really have are moments of introspection, and coupled with a sense of wealth and education money cannot buy.

Her Name Was Arabic

The fragrant oils found in the Middle East endeared themselves to me very soon after arriving in the region. Of the merchants lined up outside the locals mosques after prayer was always a young boy selling his own perfume oils made with the richest scents I've ever come across. The oils had the magical ability to bring about the most subtle and calming moods forever making themselves staples in my life. When I returned home to had a tote bag full of amazing fragrances which I cherished deeply. The scents of the Arabs had come home with me.

There were quite a few aspects of Arab culture I adopted, namely the mannerisms when dealing with guests and travelers, however, the main thing from the Arab people that I made myself intimate with was their language. As soon I set foot in the Saudi Arabia I commenced to pick up the tongue of the locals which was no easy task. The Arabic language is arguably the most difficult language in the world. In addition to a totally new alphabet, there are sounds in Arabic that are not found in English. Despite the difficulties I grew to love the Arabic language as it reminded me of a beautifully complicated yet simple woman who would only open up to those who worked tirelessly to understand her ways. To me, this was the Arabic language in a nutshell.

Learning a new language is quite the task. As with any other skill, the new language learner must be dedicated to mastering the target language. My first 9 months in Saudi Arabia were spent studying Arabic in upwards of 8 hours a day. My study regiment began shortly after dawn during which I would memorize various texts in the Arabic. The memorization drills aided in developing my tongue to be able to properly pronounce those sounds which were not in my mother tongue. Hour after hour I recited sentences and paragraphs over and over until I perfected the many sounds originating from the throat. Tiresome to say the least, the drills often left me with a sore throat which necessitated a cup of hot tea be present at all times while studying. After time had passed I had become very good at properly pronouncing all the Arabic sounds making it the first of many mountains which would eventually to be climbed.

Much of my time was also spent delving into Arabic grammar as well as the other language skills such as listening, writing and listening. My pursuit of mastering Arabic soon became a burning obsession that consumed me day and night. Perhaps the urgency of being in an Arabic country and needing to converse spearheaded my inspiration to learn the language.

Being that people are naturally social beings, I was at a great social disadvantage due to the language barrier. Simple requests at the super markets were a task which became increasingly frustrating, so I had no choice aside from working tirelessly to understand what the locals were saying. From dawn to dusk, Arabic was all I was concerned with. The walls of my study were plastered with phrases and grammar rules. My nights often ended with my trusty Arabic dictionary laying on my chest as I dozed off while studying. Learning a second had become my past-time as well as my passion. Due to this incessant drive and hunger I progressed very quickly with Arabic. While I had difficulties understanding many of the dialects, I was soon able to delve into Arabic books which brought about a sense of achievement that empowered me.

Researchers have stated that learning a second language makes a person smarter. While intelligence is very subjective, I can attest to feeling, what I consider to be, smarter. My analytical thinking skills increased dramatically because the second language forced me to think, listen, and speak differently. In Arabic the sentence structure is not like English. The language is so malleable that one idea can be conveyed in a multitude of ways which makes the speakers sharper due to having to pick which construction is most suitable to the conversation. The listener is also forced to tune in closely because of the many different ways a simple sentence such as, "David is riding the bike" can be expressed. The feeling was almost like listening to numerous radio programs simultaneously with the hopes of catching on to one station with clarity while still listening for the other stations. Daunting and overwhelming best describes the struggle of learning to listen to a new language. On many days I developed massive headaches I could only treat with a healthy dose of sleep. Maybe it was mental exhaustion or perhaps my brain was really malfunctioning due to an overload. Nevertheless, my listening activities made me much more a keen listener, in general, not just with my second language.

Arabic is an extremely precise language. A slight error in pronunciation can change the meaning for the worse as is the case in the following sentences:

You are my heart.
You are my dog.

While these sentences sound nothing alike in English, in Arabic they are quite close phonetically making a statement of endearment prone to be mispronounced and misunderstood as an insult. Because of this, attention to detail becomes a skill that language learners must pick up.

Prior to the Arabic language I wasn't very detail orientated; however, the language pushed me to grow in that regard.

The overall process of language learning had also led to me to continuing my education. My mind felt open and new, eager for more input. My logic was: "If I can learn the hardest language in the world, then studying subjects in my mother tongue should be a breeze." In order to test my theory out I signed up for tutorials on Khanacademy.org. Throughout high school I had always had difficulties grasping upper level math, so I set out to learn what eluded me in my youth. To my surprise, subjects such as algebra and geometry where incredibly easy to grasp despite the fact I had not gone over those subjects since high school. I felt smarter which led to me doing smarter things.

Unfortunately, my command of Arabic has weakened since returning to America. Not being submersed in an Arabic world has had its negative effects, but despite this I still make conversation whenever I come across an

Arab in New York City. In the future, I intend to pick up Spanish just for the sake of nurturing the skill of learning a new language. Moving forward, I intend to live on every livable continent and continuing my education to a post graduates level; both aspirations are direct results of leaving my American comfort zone. Once I left my familiar surroundings, I learned new things about myself I wasn't aware of before becoming an expatriate. Traveling coupled with learning a second language grew me in ways I am still discovering with each day that passes.

Made in the USA
Middletown, DE
31 December 2020